Jade

COLLECTORS' BLUE BOOKS

Jade

LOUIS ZARA

WALKER AND COMPANY, NEW YORK

For Marlene

Page 1: FIG. 1 Chinese ox. Pale grayish-green. Han. 3¾ × 7¼ × 3⅜ in. M. H. de Young Memorial Museum, San Francisco, Avery Brundage Collection.

FRONTISPIECE: Chinese holed disk (*Pi*). Once green, now off-white to light grayish-beige, with hint of gray-green. Late Eastern Chou, Period of the Warring States, 481–422 B.C. 6½ in. diameter. Nelson Gallery—Atkins Museum, Kansas City.

Page 6: FIG. 2 Jadeite mask from Valley of Central Mexico. Light green flecked with darker green. "Teotihuacán III style," Classic period, ca. A.D. 300–500. 5½ × 5½ in. Seattle Art Museum.

Library of Congress Catalog Card Number: 69–15722

Published simultaneously in Canada by The Ryerson Press, Toronto

Printed in the United States of America

Designed by Joseph Bourke Del Valle

ACKNOWLEDGMENTS

TO THE FOLLOWING institutions, officials, and collectors, the special thanks of the author for many courtesies: American Museum of Natural History, New York; Art Institute of Chicago, Chicago; Auckland Institute and Museum, Auckland, New Zealand; The British Museum, London; The Brooklyn Museum, Brooklyn, N.Y.; Buffalo Museum of Science, Buffalo, N.Y.; Cleveland Museum of Art, Cleveland; M. H. de Young Memorial Museum, San Francisco; Dumbarton Oaks (The Pre-Columbian Collection), Washington, D.C.; Field Museum of Natural History, Chicago; Fogg Museum of Art, Harvard University, Cambridge, Mass.; Freer Gallery of Art, Washington, D.C.; Fundaçao Calouste Gulbenkian, Oeiras, Portugal; Metropolitan Museum of Art, New York; Minneapolis Institute of Art, Minneapolis; Museo Nacional de Antropologica, Mexico City, Mexico; Museum of the American Indian, Heye Foundation, New York; National Museum, Smithsonian Institution, Washington, D.C.; William Rockhill Nelson Art Gallery, Kansas City, Mo.; Oakland Museum, Oakland, Calif.; Peabody Museum of Archaeology and Ethnology of Harvard University, Cambridge, Mass.; Royal Ontario Museum, Toronto; The Sackler Collections, New York; Seattle Art Museum, Seattle, Wash.; Smith College Museum of Art, Northampton, Mass.; University Museum (University of Pennsylvania), Philadelphia; University Museum of Ethnology and Archaeology, Cambridge, England; Victoria and Albert Museum, London; Walker Art Center, Minneapolis; Württembergisches Landesmuseum, Stuttgart.

And to: Thomas H. Ainsworth, Miss Elizabeth P. Benson, Avery P. Brundage, Mr. and Mrs. Richard C. Bull, G. H. S. Bushnell, Frank Caro, Miss Jeanne Harris, Desmond Gure, Dr. Richard E. Fuller, Mrs. Douglas Holsclaw, Dr. Hans Klaiber, Dr. Paul Singer, Dr. Albert M. Sackler, George Van Hagen. Especially also, to my superb editor Mrs. Joan Vass.

Note: all objects are of jade. Where not otherwise indicated, the object is of nephrite. Dates arbitrarily used here for early Chinese dynasties are: Shang ca. 1523–1027 B.C., Chou ca. 1026–222 B.C., Western Chou 1026–771 B.C., Eastern Chou 770–256 B.C., Han 206 B.C.–A.D. 220.

FIG. 3   Chinese pendants: five hares, a stag and an elephant fragment. Mostly mottled green-ish-brown and tan; stag dark green with lighter markings, elephant pale green, partly calcinat-ed. Largest is hare in second row right: 1 1/16 × 2 1/4 × 1/8 in.; smallest, hare, third row: 3/4 × 1 1/8 × 1/16 in. Early Western Chou. The Art Institute of Chicago, Sonnenschein Collection.

JADE, WHICH THE CHINESE have exalted for nearly four thousand years as their "Jewel of Heaven," is still, even in the West, the mystery stone of the ages.

No precious stone has been so long revered by so many different peoples in so many widely separated regions of the earth. Long before men knew the diamond, ruby, sapphire, emerald or topaz, jade was being employed for tools and weapons, as well as for sacred objects in ritual and ceremonial. Since Neolithic times, when men first became aware of the tough, intractable, long-lasting jade, no other mineral has been so venerated, nor so often interred with the distinguished dead to accompany them into the afterlife.

To no other stone, precious or semiprecious—not even the glittering metal gold—have so many remarkable qualities been attributed in lore and legend. No other has inspired such admiration and affection.

If Americans and Europeans do not believe, as did the rulers and philosophers of old China, that in jade are embodied the five cardinal virtues—charity, modesty, courage, justice and wisdom—they value it nonetheless for its serene beauty. The continued spread of knowledge about gems and minerals, at a time when many new "finds" have brought quantities of raw jade on the market, has made it possible for more ordinary people to own *something* of jade today than even knew it existed in all the millennia before.

One of the phenomena of our affluent societies has been the growth of a modern cult of jade zealots. Never before have so many haunted auction galleries and antique shops in quest of old objects of jade, from buckles to snuffbottles. Never before have so many gone jade hunting in difficult terrain —in California skin-divers seek it in hazardous waters off the Monterey coast—and then, in home workshops, have tumble-polished the rough pebbles, or cut slabs from the boulders or carved objects from sizable blocks. Cadres of determined, and sometimes highly skilled, amateur lapidaries have produced rings, beads, cabochons, spheres, animals and figurines. In California, a group of twenty-eight dedicated "jade people," members of the San Francisco Gem & Mineral Society, spent nearly $10,000 on materials and collectively devoted about 12,000 man-hours of work, in a seven-year period, to fashion an entire clock out of jade.

What has led on the modern jade fancier has not been, necessarily, any homage to the artistry and sophistication of the old jades of China, or to the clever craftsmanship of the new; or admiration for the brutal vigor of the Olmec, Aztec and Maya jades; or the placid jades of the Maoris; or even the simple, unadorned jades of the Eskimos and their Northwest Coast Indian neighbors. It has been rather jade's own peculiar mystique, timeless, placeless. Just as it cast its spell in prehistoric times, and caused men to sort over hundreds of dull-looking pebbles in hope of finding one water-worn green nephrite, so it still enchants their twentieth-century descendants.

One enters the fellowship of jade voluntarily, often unconsciously, while "rock hunting" for jade, or handcrafting it or merely handling and fondling it. From Alaska to Wyoming, from Japan to Australia, from Guatemala to Burma, jade is where you find it, and its appeal, in pebble, boulder or polished piece, is international.

Nevertheless, there is more misinformation about jade than about any other precious, or semiprecious, stone. What is jade, which is not one mineral but two, which comes in many colors, is important enough to have imitations, is costly enough at its best to command princely sums, is common enough to be acquired by anyone, has been the object of veneration and the subject of superstition, and yet, unlike opal, has never had a whisper of the unlucky about it?

The purpose here is to present at least the minimum information: What Every Intelligent Man (or Woman) Should Know About Jade. Included will be a résumé of its curious history, a digest of the basic scientific data and a few important pointers that may make collecting it less risky, and buying it more rewarding, perhaps more profitable, in the long run.

FIG. 4   Scepters, probably badges of rank. All surfaces plain. Left to right: brownish, greenish-brown, grayish-green. Straight blade in center: 16 ⅞ × 2 ¾ × ¼ in. Others have concave edges and spurs at handle. Left: 15 ½ × 2 ⅞ × ⅜ in.; right: 14 × 3 × 5⁄16 in. Early Western Chou. The Art Institute of Chicago, Sonnenschein Collection.

FIG. 5 Arched pendants with tigerlike silhouettes. Top: both sides carved with c-scrolls, grayish-green with brown markings, glossy, $3\frac{3}{8} \times 6\frac{1}{2} \times \frac{1}{4}$ in. Bottom: plain surfaces, tail-piece broken off, pale grayish-green with tan and brown markings, somewhat discolored, $2\frac{1}{4} \times 4\frac{3}{4} \times \frac{5}{16}$ in. Late Eastern Chou. The Art Institute of Chicago, Sonnenschein Collection.

CHAPTER I

Facts and Superstitions

extreamly important paragraph [handwritten annotation]

JADE IS THE NAME applied to *two* hard, very tough minerals: *nephrite* and *jadeite*. To the mineralogist they both are metasilicates, which means that their molecules have a habit of linking in chains. Both form crystals in the monoclinic system, but their crystals are seldom seen.

Nephrite, a silicate of calcium and magnesium, is a compact-fibrous variety of the tremolite-actinolite minerals in the amphibole group. Like the others in this family, it shows, under magnification, a cross section that is approximately diamond-shaped. Some of the amphiboles are so fibrous that they can be picked off or separated easily. In nephrite, however, the crystals are matted or compressed together tightly, like the felt used for hats. This compactness, resulting from the complex integration of bundles of the thin, almost filament-like crystals, makes the mineral not merely tough but almost unbreakable.

Jadeite, a silicate of sodium and aluminum, belongs to the pyroxene group, to which also belong spodumene, diopside, enstatite and augite. Jadeite has a cleavage splinter that, under magnification, shows a square or rectangular cross section. Its crystals are shorter and granular (instead of fibrous, as in nephrite) and are closely interlocked, like a mosaic. Since jadeite is not as compact as nephrite, it is not as tough. Yet the bond is so complex and firm that the whole surface of jadeite is *harder* than nephrite.

Jadeite is also denser, or heavier. In simpler terms, nephrite is about *three* times heavier than water; jadeite is about *three and a third* times heavier than water. This difference in density, or specific gravity, permits a ready identification in a specific gravity test.

Both nephrite and jadeite are minerals of metamorphic origin, which means that they are the result of tremendous changes through heat, pressures and chemical actions, in geologic times. They are seldom found *in situ* (in place) but usually as boulders or pebbles that have washed down in the gravels that line the beds of streams. Nephrite, when in place, is associated with serpentine, which is softer, and with hornblende gneiss and schist. Jadeite, when in place, may vary in its associations, but usually is near albite feldspar, nepheline or quartzite and is surrounded by serpentine. The two jades are seldom found side by side; yet, in 1950, nephrite and jadeite were located in California in a single place at the north fork of the Eel River.

Alike, and yet not alike! In pebble form, a rough nephrite and a rough jadeite, each with an outer weathered crust, may look very much alike, although the nephrite may seem shinier, the jadeite sandier. A rounded pebble of nephrite is very difficult to break; jadeite, which is harder, fractures more easily.

A freshly broken chip of nephrite looks somewhat duller, flakier, and on thin edges will be rather translucent. Jadeite, which has a more splintery fracture, sometimes tends to split into plates. Under a lens, jadeite appears more crystalline; under very high magnification, the individual crystals can be seen. Nephrite, under the same magnification, will reveal its wavy, uneven bundles, or clusters or tufts, of filamentlike fibers.

To train the eye to tell them apart, a polished nephrite should be examined alongside a polished jadeite. The nephrite looks oily, while the jadeite looks glassy. Also, the jadeite *looks* harder than the nephrite, and seems waxy. Jadeite often shows a crystalline or scaly texture, and its surface may seem dimpled from the polishing.

Sometimes one can distinguish between them quickly, and sometimes one cannot. A jade that is the color of mutton fat is likely to be nephrite. The whitest of white jades is probably nephrite. A vivid emerald-green—like the "Imperial" green—is sure to be jadeite; no nephrite displays that intense shade of green. A malachite-green will also be jadeite. Blue-green, mauve, lilac or lavender will probably be jadeite; so will the bright tomato-red that sometimes occurs in thin layers at the outer crusts of Burmese jade boulders. Such bold colors are never seen in nephrite.

Beyond these exceptions, one dare not depend on color alone. A brown-orange, a red-brown or a yellow-brown jade can be either nephrite or jadeite. A black jade may be chloromelanite, a jadeite that contains iron, but there is a black nephrite from Wyoming, locally called "King-black," which polishes to a black mirror finish.

Eyes that have studied hundreds of jades judge the luster, the texture—the smoothness or the dimpling of it, and the intensity, or the muting, of the color. A beam of light under a polished edge may reveal the interior to be either fibrous or crystalline.

Because, normally, a rapid checking of all points must be made, it is worth memorizing the basic data:

NEPHRITE	JADEITE
Hardness: 6 to 6.5	Hardness: 6.5 to 7
	—slightly harder than nephrite
Density: 2.96 to 3.10	Density: 3.3 to 3.5
	—heavier than nephrite
Refractive Index: 1.62	Refractive Index: 1.66

Nephrite will *float* in a heavy liquid with a density of 3.

Jadeite will *sink* in a heavy liquid with a density of 3.3 (methyl iodide).

Nephrite fuses with difficulty before the flame of a blowpipe. When it does fuse, it will turn white, but it will *not* color the flame yellow, and it will not melt until *very* intense heat is applied.

Jadeite will fuse easily before the flame of a blowpipe. It will form a clear globule that seems to bubble, and the sodium in it will color the flame a bright yellow.

Nephrite when polished seems to be oily (rather than glassy).

Jadeite when polished seems to be glassy (rather than oily) and looks harder than nephrite and waxy. When polished, jadeite may also appear to have a dimpled surface.

Of the many available tests, none except the hardness test is easy for the average collector. Yet, simple as it is, the hardness check is often either forgotten or ignored. Hardly a collector has not sometime been left open-mouthed with chagrin when he casually applied the tip of his penknife to a carving that he was "sure" was jade—No question about it!—and saw the steel make a scratch mark!

On either nephrite or jadeite, the penknife (hardness about 5.5, a bit higher for a very fine steel) should ride over smoothly. If a scratch is made, examine it with a hand lens. Make sure that it is a scratch *into* the surface and not just a contact mark that will rub away with pressure from the fingers. During the polishing process many carved jades are coated with paraffin, or some similar substance, to enhance the gloss, so the knife-edge may have scored only the slick outer coating.

Chinese "tomb" jades that were altered during their long burial in the ground, or through burning, may yield to a knife blade. Yet, as investigators of Chinese jades have demonstrated, an X-ray diffraction test may reveal that the material was nephrite originally, and the piece quite old indeed.

Ideally, there should be a test for hardness—with the agreement of the seller, of course—on every jade one buys, unless a specific-gravity reading, or the result of a hardness test, accompanies the bill of sale.

Should doubts arise, most collectors go to the experts for scientific appraisal. The few dollars spent for a certification by a laboratory, like that operated by the Gemmological Institute of America in New York and in Los Angeles, primarily for the jewelry industry, or the Gemmological Association of Great Britain in London, may be the most prudent expenditure in the long run.

In its ideal state, jade, whether nephrite or jadeite, would be colorless or white. James L. Kraft, the famous American cheese manufacturer who made the search for native jade and the cutting of it in his own workshop his premier hobby, said wisely, "The endless colors of jade are the result of each stone's experience in the earth."

What experiences these must have been when the planet, after boiling and seething for hundreds of millions of years, began to cool and to contract, and the minerals finally cooked themselves into being and ran into deposits! When nephrite retained its basic calcium and magnesium silicate intact, the stone remained light, or white. When any quantity of iron replaced part of the magnesium, the result could be green, or a shade of gray or black, yellow or brown, and even a rather uncommon blue.

In jadeite, the green color could be caused by chromium replacing part of the aluminum in the basic formula. Precisely how much chromium is needed to produce the magnificent "Imperial" green, no one knows. The mauve and lavender shades may have been caused by traces of manganese or vanadium. Other minerals, in small, undetermined quantities have produced the much-coveted yellows, blues, oranges and reds.

Because conditions varied in different parts of the earth's crust, the nephrites and jadeites varied. Nephrite from Asia is not precisely like nephrite from Alaska, or from California and Wyoming. It is so much different from New Zealand nephrite that the Chinese never would accept the Maori greenstone as material for their own carvings. And, jadeite from Burma is far different from the jadeite of the Aztecs and the Mayas. "Each stone's experience in the earth" has been different.

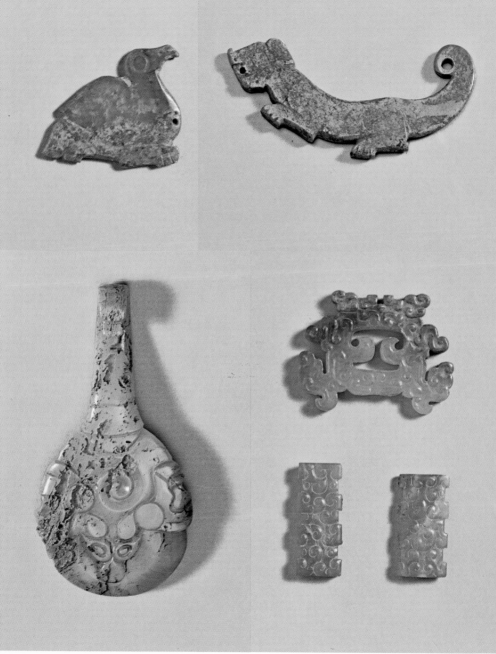

Jade stubbornly refuses to yield its secrets. From the day it is picked out of a stream bed, or dislodged from a dike, it is never easy to understand or to handle. Confronted with any jadeite boulder, jade speculators in the Orient still risk large sums on their judgments: how much precious jade, green or any other color, is imprisoned under the forbidding outer crust? Within a single pebble or boulder, many shades may lie concealed.

In Burma and Hong Kong, "windows" are cut for a glimpse into the interior of the jadeite. However, until the entire boulder has been sliced, like a large roast, the jade remains a gamble. Will the color be dull or bright? Will it be free from fractures, or will it be veined with flecks and impurities that may plague the cutter? Or will it contain that one beautiful core of green—or mauve, or yellow, or blue—that will pay for all the trouble?

"Imperial" green is, of course, very rare. Rare also is pure white jade. The Chinese say that one hundred different shades may be called "white," and yet not be the rare, true, milk-white jade. These off-whites would include the greasy-looking mutton-fat jade prized in the Orient (and little appreciated in the West); camphor jade, the color of medicinal camphor; chicken-bone jade, which looks like dried chicken bone; duck-bone jade, which looks like dried duck bone, and jade that is like curds and whey, creamy ivory or the beige of oatmeal. There is also butter-yellow jade, saffron jade and egg-yolk golden jade. There is jade as blue as the sky and, although rarely, jade that is sapphire blue; also purple, mauve and lavender jade. And amber jade, orange jade, pink jade and jade that is almost ketchup-red. And the fabulous "five-color" jade, in which, *in the same piece* (of jadeite), white, yellow, green, red and blue hues nestle against each other. However, to the public, jade is best known for its spectrum of greens: lettuce-green, grass-green, leek-green, celadon-green, apple-green, malachite-green, boiled-spinach green and greens so dark as to seem black, like chloromelanite.

Although nephrite, too, has a wide range, jadeite offers the greatest variety of colors, including the celebrated "Imperial" green. Incidentally, jadeite is by far the rarer mineral.

Both jades have unusual strength and, more tenacious than granite, are

Page 17: COLOR PLATE I   Chinese jades. Top: goose and tiger, each holed for amulet. Lower left: belt hook, unusual in jade. In profile, slender neck shows "hook" with dragon head. Reverse has stud for fastening to belt. Early Han. 4¼ × 2¼ in. Lower right: above, plaque (illustration is reversed top to bottom) with animals back to back. 1⅜ × 1½ in. Below, plaques with c-scrolls and indentations. Late Eastern Chou. The Sackler Collections, New York.

the toughest stones on earth. Big blocks of jadeite can hardly be broken up with hammers. Specimens of nephrite are said to have resisted pressure of more than 92,000 pounds to the square inch, yielding only after two hours to a stress of more than 94,000 pounds to the square inch. It would be easier to carve a billet of solid, tempered steel than a block of either jade.

What does "jade" mean? Call it the "colic stone," for the word derives from the Spanish *piedra de ijada*, or "stone for the loin." In his *Discovery of Guiana*, Sir Walter Raleigh called it *piedras hijadas*. In French, the feminine *l'ejade*, via a printer's error, became the masculine *le jade*, and entered English as "jade." In any case, the new Americas, and not the Far East, were responsible for the introduction of jade into Europe.

Early writers, translating the Spanish *piedra de riñónes* (stone for the kidneys) into Latin, rendered it *lapis nephriticus*. It was officially named nephrite by the German mineralogist A. G. Werner in 1789. And nephrite it remained for more than seventy years.

That there were two jade minerals was first discovered by the French chemist Augustine Alexis Damour. Comte Klaczkowsky, who was in Peking in 1860 during the sacking of the Summer Palace, had brought back to Paris several unusual emerald-green jades. Albert Jules Jacquemart, the ceramics authority, called them "*Jade Imperial*" because the color was as vivid as the splendid green on the Imperial porcelains. Then Damour announced that the beautiful jade was *not* nephrite at all. If it was not, what was it? For beauty and hardness it certainly was worthy of the honorable name. *Two* jades? So it seemed. Damour, in 1863, observing that the new jade was like the jade of the Aztec and Maya carvings, named it jadeite. And so the *piedra de ijada* of Cortez became jadeite.

The new name may not have been a happy choice. That nephrite is the original jade of Asia and that jadeite is the later jade originally found in the New World—and only two and a half centuries later in Burma—seems confusing, but it is true.

Until about 1780, the only jade used in China was nephrite. That does not mean that jadeite was never seen inside that vast China prior to that date. For several centuries, Kachin tribesmen had been picking jadeite pebbles and boulders from the gravel beds near the headwaters of the Chindwin and Mogung tributaries of the Irawaddy River and bartering them to Chinese

FIG. 6 Pig, may have been shroud weight. Simple cuts indicate limbs, eyes, ears and exaggerated snout. Green, calcified areas. Han. 4 in. long. The Metropolitan Museum of Art, New York.

traders across the Burmese border. Ch'ien-lung (1711–1799), the Manchu emperor-connoisseur, paid well for the vivid greens. It was not until about 1780 that supplies of the new jade became dependable via a regular traffic through Canton.

Nephrite is not easy to polish and seldom polishes brilliantly. It has a tendency to "undercut." Often it seems ready to bring up a polish when, suddenly, it roughens. Soft spots in the mineral cause this. When all the fibers lie perpendicular to the surface, there is no problem. But the fibers may lie parallel to the surface, or they may lie criss-cross. When they lie parallel the filamentlike fibers may be picked off by the abrasive. The weakening of the structure causes the "undercutting."

Jadeite is more crystalline, and is more likely to fracture. It is also a bit harder, and can scratch nephrite. Its surface, with its many crystals, some parallel and some at right angles, can give the lapidary a hard time, but, in the main, it is easier to polish than nephrite.

Anyone who has ever seen a bead of pure emerald jade from Burma ("*Jade Imperial!*") will not soon forget it. Or a droplet of lavender jade; or the "moss in snow" that looks like green lichen peering through melted icy slush; or the translucent red that spreads like carnelian on a pure white background. Such colors in Burmese jade are exciting. That jadeite was different could not have escaped the notice of Ch'ien-lung, and certainly not that of his craftsmen.

When men cut, slab, carve and polish jade day after day, they become intimate with its nature. A casual buyer could be deceived, not the Chinese lapidaries who lived with it. However, it was not their task to cry, "Old jade!" or "New jade!" Jade is jade. The Burma material was superb.

A few of the more common superstitions about jade are worth noting because they are still accepted in many quarters:

1. *Jade protects against disease, especially ailments of the groin and the kidneys.* The Aztecs believed it had a prophylactic effect in gastric pains and the passing of gravel. Bernal Díaz del Castillo, the young soldier-historian who was eyewitness to the triumph of Cortez, declared that four jades he had obtained helped heal his wounds and gather his food!

   In 1569, less than a half-century after the first jades from the New World could have circulated in Europe, Niccolo Monardes wrote that "the so-called nephritic stone is a species of stone, the finest of which resemble the emerald crystal, and are green with a milky hue. . . . This stone has an occult property by means of which it exercises a wonderful prophylactic effect, preventing the occurrence of nephritic pain, and should it nevertheless ensue, removing or alleviating it."

   Sir Walter Raleigh observed that the "Amazones" exchanged large plates of gold for "a kinde of greene stone" which they used against discomforts of the spleen. The belief that jade was effective against gallstones and kidney stones apparently derived from the fact that jade was so hard that it could break up any other stones. So the legends multiplied. In one place jade was cited for a triumph over biliousness and disordered blood. In another it was praised for checking hemorrhages. In a third it was considered potent for reducing edema in the feet.

   In the Ming dynasty, the Chinese pharmacopoeia offered a "divine liquor" of jade that refreshened the blood, calmed the mind, enriched the spirit, soothed the muscles and nourished the bones. The grains passed through the intestines; only the *virtue* of the jade filtered into the body!

   One prescription, purported to relieve heartburn, asthma and thirst, was good also for the voice and kept the hair glossy. The apothecary was cautioned to grind only fresh jade: any that had lain in a tomb might have "altered" and so have been contaminated. Physicians were warned that overdosing might reduce effectiveness should the jade be needed in a serious emergency!

2. *Jade retards the decomposition of the body.* As early as the fourth century, the Chinese began to block the nine orifices of the corpse with special amulets and plugs of jade (FIGS. 7, 8) to stay putrefaction. A cicada of jade was deposited on the tongue; almond-shaped covers of jade were laid over the eyes; holed disks of jade were placed under the back and on the chest. Sometimes pigs of jade were sewn into the shroud to hold it firm. The body of a man who had, over a period of time, imbibed nearly five pounds of jade was said not to have changed color after death and, when exhumed several years later, to be as fresh as ever.

Taoist philosophers maintained that, under proper conditions, swallowing jade might enable one to live a thousand years, or to become invisible and to fly through the air!

The Aztecs fixed a bit of jade on the dead man's tongue, as if to replace with it the life that had been stilled within. South Sea Islanders eagerly swallowed finely powdered jade before they died to prevent subsequent decay of the body.

3. *Jade brings good fortune.* Vendors of jade seldom dispute this. Anyone who owns jade may say he feels better for it. No wonder, since jade has been the beneficiary of more word-of-mouth praise than any other stone.

To the Chinese it was the quintessence of the creative force. To the Mayas, according to one writer, it was "a symbol and a passion." The Eskimos carried talismans of jade when they went hunting or fishing. The members of a certain Moslem sect carried a flat jade from birth to death. On the Loyalty Islands in the South Pacific, men were ready to trade their daughters for a necklace of jade beads.

In England the story circulated that when the horse Cicero won the Derby, his owner, Lord Rosebery, had his lucky jade amulet in his purse. On another occasion, Lord Rothschild wore *his* lucky jade and his St. Amand won the Derby. It is irreverent to speculate what might happen if every owner wore a jade amulet; probably the best jade would win.

FIGS. 7 and 8 Above: cicada, symbol of rebirth. Greenish-white with glossy surface. Late T'ang or Sung, 10th–13th century A.D. 2 × 1 ¼ × ⅞ in. Below: eye covers. Convex on top, flat on bottom. Holes for sewing to face-covering of dead. White, calcified. Han. 1 × 2 in. and 1 × 2 ¹⁄₁₆ in. Smith College Museum of Art, Northampton, Mass., Hart Collection.

CHAPTER II

China

JADE, WHETHER FOUND in Burma, Alaska, Wyoming, California, Taiwan, Japan, Mexico, Guatemala, Rhodesia or Australia still conjures images of China and what jade meant to the life and philosophy of that people.

Confucius, who lived in the sixth century B.C., said that in ancient times superior men found the likeness of all excellent qualities in jade: soft and smooth yet gleaming, like benevolence; fine, compact and strong, like intelligence; unyielding yet not sharp and cutting, like righteousness; lowly, like humility; sonorous, for when struck it yields a note, like music; its flaws never conceal its beauty nor does its beauty hide its flaws, like loyalty; its radiance issues from every side, like good faith; its brightness is like the rainbow's, like heaven; its exquisiteness is in the hills and the streams, like earth; it attracts attention as a symbol of rank, like virtue; and it is esteemed by all under the light of the sun, like the path of truth and duty.

In Confucius' time, there was already a millennium-old tradition of the veneration of jade. Its substance was both virtue and the receptacle of virtue, like honey and the comb in which it is stored. Its color, feel and sound were merely extended proofs of its interior nobility. *Yü*, the word for jade, became a synonym for beauty, physical as well as spiritual. Thus, a beautiful woman was "a woman of jade," a handsome man had a "countenance like jade" and the highest Taoist divinity was called "the Jade Emperor."

Where did the Chinese obtain their jade? No one can say. If the mountains within the Eighteen Provinces of the Middle Kingdom ever yielded jade, those sources had long been depleted. The only dependable regions for jade were in what is now Sinkiang province, then called Turkestan. Khotan and Yarkand became famous for the splendid blocks of jade they sent to the emperors from their mountain quarries and riverbeds.

FIG. 9   Ceremonial implement. Jade blade set in bronze handle inlaid with turquoise mosaic. Mottled gray-brown and white, scattered malachite incrustations. From An-yang, Honan province. Late Shang. 8⅜ × 3⅛ in. Freer Gallery of Art, Washington, D.C.

FIG. 10   Shang arrowheads, spearhead, knife and hoe blade. Perhaps ceremonial. Arrowheads (each over 2 in. long) and spearhead, 6¼ × 1 ⅞ × ¼ in., could have been used. Dark-green knife blade, probably funerary gift, 3 ³⁄₁₆ × 1 ⅛ × ³⁄₁₆ in. Hoe blade has cutting edges, 5 ¹⁄₁₆ × 2 ½ × ⁵⁄₁₆ in. The Art Institute of Chicago, Sonnenschein Collection.

Jade had entered Chinese life in Neolithic times as the material par excellence for tools and weapons (FIG. 10). When the old animistic beliefs crystallized into a broad worship of nature, jade, with its manifold virtues, became absorbed into the religious awareness. In the process it acquired a unique significance and a highly charged symbolism that caused it to appeal to many different sensibilities. Agriculture, religion and war—the three great forces in society—were embraced and ennobled by it. When formalization drained the dynamism from the old rituals and ceremonies, jade, too, was robbed of its mythological meaning. But by then it had so permeated the national, or racial, consciousness that its existence per se had a personal value for everyone, from emperor to farmer.

We do not understand the full rich intentions in the earliest Chinese jades. What must once have been so clear is obscured: the Chinese themselves have not penetrated all the cryptic meanings. What can be said is that we *believe* we have grasped the essential symbolism.

Objects of jade were employed in the worship of the supreme deities of Heaven and Earth and the Four Cardinal Points of Direction. Heaven was circular, as the sky appeared to be, while Earth, with its "four corners," was rectangular. The Ruler stood between Heaven and Earth, and between the People and the Supreme Power. Rituals accompanied all their communications, and emblems of jade graced the occasions when these rites were performed in public worship (FIGS. 4, 9).

The essential shapes in jade were: the circular holed disk called *Pi* (pronounced bee), which stood for Heaven; the squared hollow tube, cylindrical inside, which was called *Ts'ung*, and represented Earth; the green tablet called *Kuei*, which represented the deity East and was, later, a token of rank; the flattish holed ring called *Huan*, which represented the deity North; the red scepter-blade called *Chang*, which represented the deity South; and the tiger tablet called *Hu*, which represented the deity West; also, the dagger-ax called *Ko*, which was a ritual weapon; and the peculiar arc called *Huang*, which was either a half-*Pi* or, occasionally, a third-*Pi*.

Jade supplied a precious link with the past. Long after jade adzes and hoes, and daggers and halberds had ceased to be used, they remained as noble memorials to the blessed Beginnings, and were carried or worn by worthy persons in pageant and parade. Later, when rank and ceremony became so important, jade denoted the first and helped to sanctify the second.

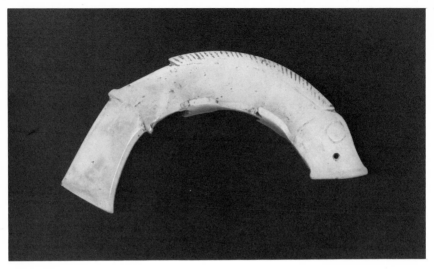

FIG. 11 Semicircular pendant, identical both sides. Once green, now calcified. Late Eastern Chou. ¾ × 4 × ⅛ in. Smith College Museum of Art, Northampton, Mass., Hart Collection.

Did not the emperor himself wear jade sandals? Did he not worship before a jade altar, with the jade scepter-blade *Chang* tied to his girdle? Jade expressed his power; jade emphasized his commands. Jade served as the official warrant of a position; jade signaled the nature of an imperial purpose, religious or military. The imperial seal and baton were both of jade.

Since jade was so desirable for the emperor and his circle, it surely must be beneficial to the lesser members in his entourage. Court officials proudly wore jade insignia for emblems of rank. Even lower personages attached amulets and talismans of jade to their garments. They coveted ornaments of jade for all whom they loved dearly: aged parents, eldest children, adored mistresses.

No wonder that at burial the body was surrounded with as many jades as a man's wealth permitted and his family's pride demanded. Only thus was tranquillity ensured in the dark of the grave, with sweet odors enveloping the cold rigid flesh.

"Acts of the greatest reverence require no ornament," wise men maintained. The jades therefore were plain, thin and highly polished, but otherwise unadorned. From the earliest periods, the blades of jade—1/4, 1/8 or even 1/16 inch thick—are unbelievably fragile and unbelievably tough. Even today, no diamond-charged saw can deliver whole any blades longer or more amazingly

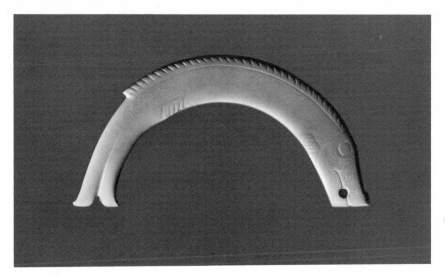

FIG. 12   Semicircular pendant. Chicken-bone white. Early Western Chou. 3 %₁₆ in. long.
Cleveland Museum of Art.

thin than those the Chou lapidaries could produce.

Except for the large, bold *Pi*, and the tall, impressive *Ts'ung*, the jades in
the early dynasties were small and simple. Ornamentation came later. As the
skills of the carvers increased, injunctions to reserve jade only for the nobility
became of little avail. Now, in addition to the religious symbols, the badges of
office and the funerary objects and talismans, a myriad of purely ornamental
jades were created for the pleasure of ownership: necklaces, girdle hooks,
scabbard slides and other sword fittings, plus dozens of carvings of animals,
fishes, birds, insects and fantastic creatures.

Of course, the elaborate beautification of the mineral was a tribute to it.
Jade is worked with abrasion, patience and skill, in about equal parts. The
early jade carver entered into a spiritual marriage with the material and
jealously kept its lines virginal. The later carver, especially in the Late
Eastern Chou dynasty (770–256 B.C.), lavished on his beloved jade a joy and
a skill unheard of in most of the other arts, as if he had an erotic relationship to
the difficult stone, whose nature it was to resist but which became even more
beautiful after it yielded.

The cult significance of jade would not tolerate careless or sloppy work.
That is why there are no poor Shang, or poor Chou, jades. If any substandard

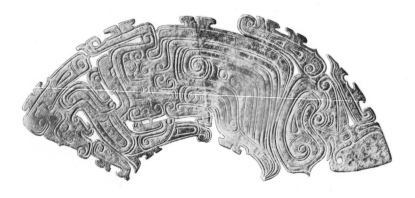

Opposite, above: FIG. 13   Holed disk (*Pi*),
engraved on both sides with fantastic
animals. Light green. Early Western Chou.
9⅝ in. diameter. Seattle Art Museum,
Eugene Fuller Memorial Collection.

Below: FIG. 14   Arched plaque in form of
fantastic animal with dragon crest. Yel-
lowish-white, calcified, traces of cinnabar in
thread lines. Perhaps Shang or Chou. 6⅝ ×
2⅞ × ¼ in. Nelson Gallery—Atkins Museum, Kansas City.

Right: FIG. 15   Handle or tablet in black-
ish- and grayish-brown, carved with inter-
twined and swarming hooks and scrolls.
Narrow hole drilled through entire length.
Late Eastern Chou. 5¾ × 1¼ × ¼ in.
Cleveland Museum of Art, John L. Sever-
ance Fund.

pieces ever issued from a worker's hands, they were promptly set aside to be cut down and refashioned into other objects. Occasionally, "tomb" jades have been found that are marvelously finished on one side but unworked on the other. But that was done on purpose; the side that is finished is of the perfect quality we expect, the other was sewn to the shroud. Only in amulets and in talismans is there ever any evidence of the crude or the unfinished, and these objects may have been made privately, from discarded or stolen fragments. Generally, any jade that does not reveal the *finished* artistry of its particular style-period must be condemned as "suspicious," *i.e.*, carved at a later date as an "archaism" or as a reproduction, or simply a downright forgery.

The basic jade-working tools—sand abrasive, rotary blade and pointed drill, either of bone or bamboo—were in use from early times. Improvements in technique and the usual "shortcuts" that craftsmen happen upon in every field were passed on, but no startling innovations for abrading (which, after all, is the fundamental operation) were introduced until carborundum and the diamond drill appeared.

The carver progressed from line engraving to relief work, and then to countersink relief. He moved from simple designs with linear patterns to the more complicated ones, where lozenges and scrolls were interlaced and interwoven. The rationale of the various motifs eludes us today. Are the raised nipples on the *Pi* representative of grains, or, with little comma tails added, are they silkworm grubs, or are they bosses repeated from battle shields? Are the interlocked c-scrolls abstract silkworm larvae or cocoons?

What attracts us is the vigor of the carving. The thread lines (FIG. 14) are not easy for the modern lapidary. Those distorted bird and animal designs (FRONTISPIECE and FIG. 5), produced with masterful strength, would be admirable done in pen and ink, or etched in soft steel or copper; they are astonishing on the intractable surface of nephrite.

Observe the bird shape of green nephrite (FIG. 16) from the Neolithic period. It is unmistakably Bird. Observe the smaller green nephrite pebble that was shaped into a bird about five hundred years later (FIG. 17). Glance at the little reptile from the Shang period (FIG. 18) and the turtle (FIG. 20), probably from the same era; also the fine long fish (FIG. 19). These are not religious items, yet it is obvious that the fourth ingredient the carver applied, after patience, abrasion and skill, was affection for the object.

One of the supreme accomplishments of the Late Eastern Chou period,

FIGS. 16 and 17   Left: bird carved from green nephrite pebble, found at Neolithic site near T'ai-yuan, Shansi province. Perhaps 3rd millennium B.C., carved before metal tools were available. 4⅛ × 5½ × 2¾ in. Nelson Gallery—Atkins Museum, Kansas City. Right: bird carved from green bird-shaped pebble, probably before 13th century B.C. M. H. de Young Memorial Museum, San Francisco, Avery Brundage Collection.

when jade carving was at its height, is the *Pi* that is in the William Rockhill Nelson Gallery of Art in Kansas City (FRONTISPIECE). It has two crested tigers stalking on the rim and, in the center, an openwork medallion surmounted by the attenuated figure of a third tiger, which, scrolled around the inner ring, holds the entire jade together. Its greatest width (including the tigers) is only 8⅝ inches. Found in Honan province, in 1929, at Chin-t'sun, about ten miles east of old Lo-yang, the ancient Chou capital, no archaic jade like it has ever been discovered.

The surface is peppered with raised comma-curls that must have been difficult to abrade and to space perfectly. Each is a small erect nipple about ¹⁄₁₆ inch in diameter, with a tail incised at the root. To make a single one rise about ¼ inch from the surface would tax any lapidary's patience. Yet, on this *Pi* there are four hundred and ninety-eight raised comma-curls on each side, or just under one thousand for the entire disk.

These comma-curls are fixed in as orderly an array as if they were plants in an orchard. A raised rim guards the circumference, another the inner plaque that juts against the engirdling tiger. The central medallion has its own borders and is incised with a band of interlocked scrolls instead of comma-curls.

FIG. 18   Reptile with quasi-human mask, hind quarters notched and pointed. Carving on upper side in double lines, underneath in single lines. Light brown on back, green on underside. Shang. 4⅞ in. long. Dr. Paul Singer, Summit, N.J.

FIG. 19   Fish of pale green, some cinnabar adhering. Tail fin extended with chisel-like "rudder." May be Shang. 3⅜ in. long. Dr. Paul Singer, Summit, N.J.

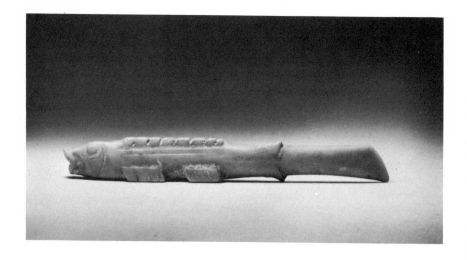

FIG. 20   Turtle with diamond designs on carapace. Now chicken-bone white. Shang. Dr. Paul
Singer, Summit, N.J.

FIG. 21   Buckle, or pair of plaques, with crested tiger and phoenix, coupled by freely moving
cylinder link. Carved from single piece of light green and brown nephrite. From Lo-yang,
Honan province. Late Eastern Chou. 3¾ × 1¼ in. Fogg Art Museum, Harvard University,
Cambridge, Bequest of Grenville L. Winthrop.

However, what truly distinguishes this *Pi* is the animal art. The tigers that pace the rim are bold, arrogant creatures, insolently aquiver with motion. The larger animal is heraldic, flaunting a curved crest, unleashing over his forepaws some sinuous protuberance that unfolds like a plume and, even from his broken tail, brandishes sheer menace.

The tiger that precedes him may be his female. She, too, with fangs bared and eyes glaring, is demonic, yet committed to an incredible rhythm. One not merely sees them, one *hears* them moving over this wheel.

The third tiger scrolls his body around the inner ring. Head twisted back, torso thrust out and curved under, his hindlegs grip desperately, while the tail curls out, rises and falls, and rises again to control the circular space. Is he the Underworld Sentinel, while the other two stalk the Overworld?

Was this *Pi* made to worship Heaven, or to declare that its owner was an official of high degree? We do not know. With an irregular slab of lovely nephrite before him, the lapidary visualized a *Pi* surmounted by elegant beasts and "invented" them in jade.

From the same period of masterpieces came the hinged plaques in the shape of a crested tiger and phoenix (FIG. 21), also said to be from Lo-yang. Two rectagonal frames side by side are linked by a broad ring—and all *of one piece of jade*: no joint in the ring, no break in the two frames. The ring moves

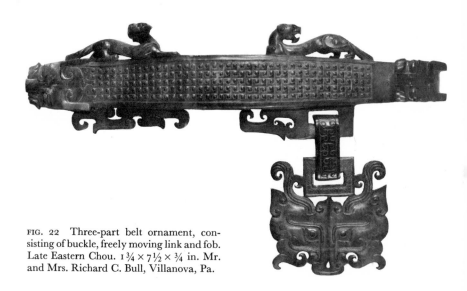

FIG. 22   Three-part belt ornament, consisting of buckle, freely moving link and fob. Late Eastern Chou. 1¾ × 7½ × ¾ in. Mr. and Mrs. Richard C. Bull, Villanova, Pa.

freely, and the frames move freely, a tiger on one, a phoenix on the other. The crested tiger crouches, talons gripping, great tail flung behind him, the majestic head thrown back, the savage jaws almost slavering. The phoenix, too, is alive, clutching, glaring.

Still another masterwork is the three-part buckle carved without a break from a single piece of reddish-brown jade (FIGS. 22, 23). The long, narrow major portion has the typical rounded end with eared dragon head, overlooking a panel with five vertical rows, each containing raised c-scrolls, each squared off, the piece concluding in a magnificent monster mask of the type called *t'ao-t'ieh*. Above, on the ledge of the buckle, two tigers sprawl regardant but with heads looking back over their shoulders. Below are two bird-curved hooks. From one hangs a small vertical strap buckle that, carved completely loose, holds a squared frame from either side of which unfolds the most graceful *t'ao-t'ieh* mask known to me in jade. It is only about 2 inches square. Horns are scrolled, nostrils are engrossed, eyes stare out.

Another buckle (FIG. 24), 3¼ inches long, is an animal sculpture of the Han dynasty (206 B.C.–A.D. 220). On the inclined slope of the rounded buckle, which is alive with incised c-scrolls, a charming little fawn is stretched. Forelegs and hindlegs thrust out, little belly and haunches slightly raised, he seems caught in flight. The ears are like bell-trumpets. The body was modeled by

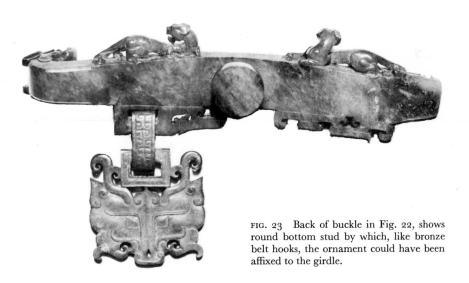

FIG. 23   Back of buckle in Fig. 22, shows round bottom stud by which, like bronze belt hooks, the ornament could have been affixed to the girdle.

FIG. 24   Fawn or antelope belt hook with stud for fastening. Han.
1½ × 3¼ in. Fogg Art Museum, Harvard University, Cambridge,
Bequest of Grenville L. Winthrop.

hands that, many a time, must have held a fawn, and felt its pulses beating.

Few large carved jades are available from the early dynasties. One of the most famous is the horse's head and neck (FIG. 26), 7½ inches high, of that grayish-green nephrite described as "glaucous." Though the mass is a dull, oily green, it is not inert. Beneath the surface an inner light seems to roll.

This jade is in two parts: the head and U-arched neck in one piece, fitted into a shoulder base that bulges where it may have joined the forepart of a large horse torso. Both pieces were cut from the same block, at least from adjacent areas. Strongly stylized, the piece represents the Horse rather than any particular steed. Once thought to resemble Han mortuary clay figures of horses' heads, and so accredited to the Han dynasty, it is now believed to be a later work, from the T'ang period (618–906).

A more likely Han candidate is another jade horse's head (FIG. 25). This one, too, is stylized, made in two pieces and shows the animal panting. However, it reveals rare equine vigor. The magnificent arch of the neck, the squaring off of the head and the gaping jaws bespeak a brute force that the other horse lacks.

This creature may have been inspired by the Ferghana steeds, then newly introduced into China. In 126 B.C., Chang Ch'ien, returning from twelve years of exploration, brought back a few of the horses he had admired in central Asia, on the silk route to the West. From such "heavenly horses," a passion with the Chinese, were bred thousands of cavalry mounts.

This fiercely regal head in jade, with its powerful neck and jaws, may be of that Ferghana breed. It should sit on a barrel-shaped body over tapering legs and slender hooves, but it was probably never intended to be a complete jade

FIG. 25 Horse's head from Han dynasty tomb. Variegated green. Adhesions remain of wood, stain and cinnabar. Neck socket is filled with metal tang. 5⅛ in. high. Fogg Art Museum, Harvard University, Cambridge, Bequest of Grenville L. Winthrop.

FIG. 26 Horse's head, two parts, carved from a single block of grayish-green nephrite. Once attributed to Han dynasty, now believed to be later work, probably T'ang, 618–906. 7½ in. high. Victoria and Albert Museum, London.

animal; it may have been fitted into a carved wooden body that was painted, or perhaps lacquered and gilded.

During the T'ang and the Sung dynasties (618–906, and 960–1279), a period of national splendor and sophistication, jade was carved vigorously (FIGS. 7 and 26), but the end was pleasure rather than spiritual enrichment. Jade, being plentiful, was the captive of the lapidary. The objects he made conscript our admiration, ranging as they do from a jade bed for Yang kuei-fei, concubine of the T'ang emperor Huan-tsung, to jade flutes. Ironic that now, when the carver was demonstrating complete command over jade and could do with it as he pleased, jade became secularized. In the Buddhist religion, which was now important in China, it never occupied the place it had in the old nature worship. However, although jade had lost its meaning as a venerated substance, the *tradition* of veneration persisted another thousand years.

The jade industry not only produced great craftsmen, it also embraced new abrasives and ingenious procedures. In the Ming dynasty (1368–1644) one whole factory within the palace precincts was devoted to the creation of the curved jade *jui* scepters, which had become very popular. The possession of jade was no longer limited to persons in high places; lesser officials, too, could enjoy it—if they could afford it. Jade remained a gift that conferred honor on the receiver and implied high taste in the donor. Available were: trays, vases, coupes, beakers, bowls, cups, ewers, flower stands, brush washers, wine pots, jewel cases, hatstands, scholars' screens, lanterns, garden seats, and miscellaneous boxes and ornaments.

The emperor Ch'ien-lung (1736–1796) even had "books" of jade. One, now in the Chester Beatty Library in Dublin, consists of fifty-three tablets of green nephrite, each 9½ by 3½ inches. Jade tablets for the inscription of permanent documents were first used at the special *Feng* and *Shan* sacrifices offered to Heaven and Earth by the emperor on the summit of Tai-shan. For these occasions prayer and decree were engraved on jade tablets that varied from 8 or 9 inches long to 4 or 5 inches wide. The "documents" were piled one on top of the other and, protected by additional jade slabs, were tied with gold cords and placed in coffers of sandalwood, stone or jade.

In 206 B.C., Kao-tsu, first Han emperor, announced his accession by sacrificing with a bright white jade tablet that was spotted with "green moss" as well as with red, blue and black. Two centuries later, Han emperor Kuang-wu (A.D. 25) sought a solid blue jade tablet for his sacrifice. The T'ang dynasty emperor T'ai-tsung (626–650) decreed that *only* jade should be used in the *Feng* and *Shan* rites. In 1008, when the emperor Chen-Tsung made his sacrifices, he required seventeen oblong slabs of jade. In 1747 these were found on Tai Mountain in two book-boxes.

More common than books of jade were the "mountains" of jade. One of the most prized Chinese jades in the United States, and perhaps the largest sculptured jade in the West, is the "Walker Mountain" (FIG. 27). Nearly 2 feet high, more than 3 feet wide, and 1½ feet deep, it weighs 640 pounds. Its color is that soft olive-green described as "light celadon," after the famous Sung dynasty celadon porcelains. The nephrite, seamed with several opaque gray veins, is alive, considering the great size, with a quiet, green coolness. The single block was quarried from a mountain in Khotan, lowered carefully to the valley and dispatched on the 2,000-mile journey to Peking on a vast sled drawn by teams of animals.

Ch'ien-lung ordered it carved as a mountain. How long the work took we do not know, or how many pairs of hands labored over the olive-green mass, which originally weighed at least 800 pounds. But now, the craggy hump does rise like a mountain in one of China's great paintings. On a flat table rock, where a brook flows, five poets are conversing. Not far away, five more are stepping gingerly on a narrow path; others idle in the shadows. The opposite side of the mountain offers a sparser scene: another sheer wall and a few straggling figures ascending on the paths. On the first wall, high above the poets, an inscription explains the scene in the emperor's strong calligraphy and dated for the spring of 1784. On the back, a Ch'ien-lung poem, also inscribed in his calligraphy, has the imperial seal affixed in red. "Only from Khotan could a jade be brought large enough to make this mountain," states the poem. The other inscription: "Not from ancient times has there been such an emperor."

Mountains for the rich, ordinary amulets and toggles for the less blessed. The toggle was merely a button with two holes, a tie-together piece for the girdle cord. (The Japanese netsuke is its nearest relative.) It was, of course, made of common substances—wood, bone, horn and ivory—and less often of precious materials, including jade. In some were combined a variety of symbols borrowed from Buddhism and Taoism.

Jade toggles that have been lovingly fondled for decades have a caressing "feel" that no lapidary's skill can improve. They come in all colors, in all shapes, some with meaning, some without. Some toggles repeat the motifs that were produced on the great jades from the Ch'ien-lung workshops: the peach (immortality), the prunus blossom (longevity), the lotus (happiness), the bat (happiness), the sacred fungus (longevity), the quail (courage), the spider (joy), the pomegranate (many children), the two fishes (conjugal bliss), the stag (longevity), the crane (longevity), the magnolia blossom (feminine beauty), the bamboo (the perfect gentleman).

Among modern works, the statuette of Kwanyin (FIG. 28), 26 inches high, is noteworthy. This figure of the Buddhist Goddess of Mercy, carved from one block of jadeite around the turn of the present century, is a splendid green. In

areas there is a grayish undertone, also brilliant leaf-green, pinkish-gray and spots that look like rust under the surface, as chemically they are because they are caused by iron oxide. A dignified presentation that is regal and human rather than a goddess, the jade radiates tranquillity. The robe hangs loosely upon the firm womanly figure. On the long, full-cheeked countenance with the downcast eyelids is a dreamy expression. A superb example of the modern lapidary's skill, it has a mirror polish that is especially admirable.

Today, China continues to produce jade of splendid style and finish. However, a practiced eye can tell the new from the old. The flesh of the jade may be magnificent, but only rarely is the spirit there too.

Opposite: FIG. 27 Jade mountain in soft olive celadon-green seamed with opaque gray veins. Dated for the spring of 1784. 22½ × 38¼ × 19 in. Walker Art Center, Minneapolis.

FIG. 28 Kwanyin, Goddess of Mercy. Green jadeite with grayish undertone, areas of brilliant leaf-green and pinkish-gray, and rust spots. Highly polished surface. Late 19th or early 20th century. 26 in. high. University Museum, Philadelphia.

CHAPTER III

Middle America

WHEN THE AZTEC RULER MONTEZUMA was at the mercy of the conquistadores, he discovered quickly that nothing was as precious to them as gold. No matter how much he surrendered, the bearded white strangers wanted more. Once he tendered to Hernando Cortez several droplets of a remarkably clear green stone, which he called *chalchihuitl* (kal-kee-whee-tl). The Spaniard, who had never seen anything like it, was not pleased. In the Valley of Mexico, however, *chalchihuitl* was infinitely more valuable than gold. The pieces Montezuma gave Cortez were small, but when the light filtered through they shone like new green corn plants.

Cortez, who was after treasure of every kind, tried to understand. He greedily accepted the *chalchihuitl* because Montezuma had said, "Each stone is worth two loads of gold." But neither Cortez nor his companions ever grasped its significance. Again and again, they encountered jade in figurines, masks, carved plaques, pendants and necklaces. And they saw that when Montezuma received his chiefs he wore, in addition to a simple crown of gold, his fine jade earrings. *Chalchihuitl* obviously was precious to the Aztecs.

The green stone was jadeite—hard, tough and rare. Where it came from no one would say; perhaps no one knew. The fabled mines may have been somewhere in Mexico, or in the Guatemalan highlands or in Costa Rica. All the peoples of Middle America prized it. The best, naturally, went to the powerful, but all coveted it and traded for it when they could.

Rare, beautiful and a symbol of life, jade was sacrifice-worthy. The gods, too, rejoiced in it. Because jade was life-enriched, it was slipped into the mouths of the dead to maintain contact with the life-force. (The Mayas believed the jade would buy food in the next life.)

From the great cenote, or sacrifice well at Chichén Itzá, into which the sacred victims were flung, vast quantities of jade have been recovered—in-

FIG. 29   The "Olmec Jewel." Fine dark-green jadeite, highly polished. Olmec, ca. 1000 B.C., or later. 8⅝ in. high. The Brooklyn Museum, New York (lent by Guennol Collection).

cluding a remarkable human face mask of pieces of black and white jadeite polished and fitted into a mosaic of features so hideously alive that it ranks as one of Middle America's finest works of art. Not far away, in a special throne room concealed under El Castillo, the pyramid-temple of Kukulcan, the plumed serpent-god, stood a life-sized jaguar with open jaws. Affixed to his powerful frame were seventy-two disks of polished jade, each apple-green, a curious application of precious *chalchihuitl* to the fearsome cult-beast.

In a Mayan pyramid at Kaminaljuyu, on the outskirts of Guatemala City, a 200-pound boulder of green jadeite was found. Apparently it had been held there as a treasured reserve. When wanted for ceremonial purposes, chunks or slabs were broken or sawn off and turned over to the skilled jade workers.

At Cerro de las Mesas, seven hundred and eighty-two pieces of jade were found, including images, plaques, beads, tubes and implements; and nearby, at La Venta, five hundred pieces of "the finest Oriental quality" in color and translucence. At Chichén Itzá, a seated palanquin figure of "flawless jade," 4 inches high, was uncovered.

At Tuxtla a jadeite statuette of a bald Indian priest, which is 8 inches high, has a calendar incised on his abdomen. It was dated in a year that corresponds to our 98 B.C. Jade articles of high quality and extraordinary workmanship have been present in every sacred place where modern archeologists have searched.

No peoples *happen* to become artistic lapidaries. The natives of Middle America must have been searching for jade, working it and venerating it— even if not in the mystical fashion of the Chinese—for many centuries. To the late William F. Foshag of the Smithsonian Institution, it appeared that the carvers of the Chou dynasty (1050–256 B.C.) in China and the carvers of the Olmec culture (800 B.C.–A.D. 600) in Mexico reached the peaks of their skills in jade (the Chinese working the nephrite, the Olmecs the jadeite) at about the same time. Viewed objectively, many Mexican jades are superior for vigor and plastic imagination even to the famed Chou carvings, although seldom their equal in the treatment of details. No jades of the Shang, Chou and Han periods compare in size to the large Olmec figures and masks in jade.

Each culture has its staunch admirers. A small but growing number of scholars believe that Chinese influence, carried by seafaring traders, reached the Aleutian armpit of the North American continent—or struck directly across the mid-Pacific—and left its mark on the art of Mexico, and even of

Peru, as early as the first millennium B.C. The longer one observes certain al-most identical images and motifs in all their arts, the more persuasive the hypothesis becomes, although that is not so evident from the jades alone.

In the half-century after Cortez, the popularity of *piedras de ijada* for medi-cinal and talismanic use in Europe contributed to the absorption of hundreds, perhaps thousands, of fine Aztec jades. Shrewd traders bought everything that could pass for jade. From the Indian caciques, they particularly sought the large pieces, and especially mosaics that could be pulled apart, or broken up easily for the traffic in "stones for the loin."

The jades that survived whole reposed either in royal collections or in the coffers of the very wealthy. Most of the gifts from Aztec princes, or the loot from their inner sancta, are on so high a level of artistic expression—at their greatest not inferior to the art products of Egypt and Greece—that one regrets that the Spaniards did not spare the elite of the jade workers. However, eager to crush the pagan crafts and reduce everything native to rubble, they ob-literated the art forms and enslaved the practitioners along with tens of thousands of others. Jade, for three millennia in use—in pebbles, carvings and mosaic elaborations—overnight became a part of the tragic Mexican past, never to be revived there either as a craft or an art form.

How odd that only when the Middle American jades were beyond price in Europe did the continuing demand bring a trade in jades with Asia, and, large or small, objects of jade became valuable cargo in the caravans down the silk route and in caravels through the Indian Ocean and around the Cape of Good Hope. In this manner, the nephrite jades of China began to enter Europe regularly. But the American jadeites had preceded them.

What colors were the original jadeites of Middle America? In many instances, the finest emerald-green, as brilliant as the "Imperial" jadeite from Burma. That was called *quetzalitzli* (kay-tzal-eetz-tli), after the green feathers of the quetzal bird. There was also *quetzal-chalchihuitl* (kay-tzal-kal-kee-whee-tl), a transparent, uniformly green jadeite. The emerald-green is seen only in small objects; the other is the lesser green of most of the better Olmec jades. Ordinary *chalchihuites* (kal-kee-whee-tess) was the common green and white jadeite. There were less desirable mixtures—a forest-green, a darker green and a white jade with very little green. Cortez, though he had seen the best, embraced them all in his Inventory as "*piedras verdes*," green stones.

A wide range of colors was thus available to the Mexican lapidary. Naturally, the rarest was the emerald-green. Then the spectrum broadened into
apple-green, grass-green and the delicate green of the young corn plant; then
olive-green, pea-green and dark ivy-green. Other greens were mottled or
dappled from white to yellow. One Olmec jade has been called "blue" jade,
but it was rather a pearl-gray blue or a green intermingled with blue. Sometimes Olmec jade has the high gloss of polished chalcedony. There were also
jadeites mixed with albite and jadeites mixed with diopside, the first ranging
from whites to greens, the second covering a variety of dark greens. The dark
chloromelanite is the only variety in which celts are still found. No tools have
ever been found in the finer greens.

We are as ignorant of the sources of Middle American jade as we are of the
sources of Shang and Chou dynasty jade. To follow the trail of jade, we have
lumped together Maya, Olmec, Toltec, Mixtec, Aztec, Huastec, Totonac and
Zapotec, although their cultures were sharply differentiated and did not all
exist contemporaneously. Nor did they all utilize jade in the same way.

The Olmecs, who had been "in place" for about fourteen hundred years,
(800 B.C.–A.D. 600), consistently created the largest jade figures and masks.
The Mayas, who were "in place" nearly thirty-seven hundred years (2000 B.C.
–A.D. 1697), seldom carved jade figures or masks, but made abundant use of
jade beads, tubes, plaques and pendants for the ritual garb of their priests and
princes. Their great jade-carving days were over long before the Spaniards
appeared.

The Aztecs, the warrior-sculptors with a flair for the dramatic in everything, were comparative newcomers, having been on the scene for only four
centuries before the white men appeared and crushed their dreams, their cities
and their gods. They may have acquired their reverence for jade from their
neighbors, for on the Aztec tribute roll jade is listed among the precious com-
modities to be exacted from their vassals. They too created numberless jade
masks, plaques and pendants. The wife of Tlaloc, the rain god, was presented
as a beautiful young woman named Chalchihuitlicue, which can be translated
as "Our Lady of the Jade (or Turquoise) Skirt." Often the Aztecs glorified
the repulsive. They carved gods in terrifying aspects. The image of Xolotl,
the monster god who shepherded the dead through the netherworld, is a
fearsome sculpture in nephrite (FIG. 30).

However, there is bold realism rather than grotesqueness in the Aztec

FIG. 30   Aztec god Xolotl carved in jadeite as skeleton, enriched with symbols and glyphs. Perhaps from the Valley of Central Mexico. If Aztec, ca. 1327–1521. 9 × 4¾ in. Württembergisches Landesmuseum, Stuttgart.

FIGS. 31 and 32 Above: miniature jadeite mask of head in peaked helmet. Open mouth is cut through; back of mask hollowed out. Classic Teotihuacán period, A.D. 300–600. 2¾ × 2⅓ in. Below: jadeite bust of a woman, broken off from a statuette. Said to be Olmec, but may have been carved later, in Olmec style. 2⅝ × 1½ in. Dumbarton Oaks, Washington, D.C., Bliss Collection of Pre-Columbian Art.

carving of the seated rabbit in green jadeite (COLOR PLATE II), said to have been found at Cempoala in the district of Vera Cruz. Here Rabbit, for whom a day in the Aztec calendar was named, may be a portrait of the God of Intoxication. He was associated with good fortune and fertility, but also with Mayahuel, the goddess who symbolized the maguey plant, from which pulque was fermented. Rabbit was also associated with the moon and with the harvest. How and why Rabbit became God of Intoxication, a state regarded as a serious offense in Aztec life, is not clear. Nor is the significance of the eagle-helmeted warrior head between his knees understood, nor even the meaning of the eagle, although the Knights of the Eagle were a select warrior group among the Aztecs.

A gentler portrait is the miniature mask in bluish-green jadeite (FIG. 31) from the Classic Teotihuacán period (300–600). This face, with peaked hat, is neither threatening nor threatened. The modeling about the narrowed eyes and nose is praiseworthy when one considers how difficult it is to abrade these features. The smile, toothlessly good-humored, is almost gay.

Among the Olmec jades, special homage is due the splendid "Olmec Jewel" figurine (FIG. 29) in green jadeite. The standing figure (8⅝ inches) with large, long head, cranium compressed and flattened, mouth squared and lip curled, holds before him a chubby child with a squared head and a jaguar-mouth distortion. The "were-jaguar" countenance recalls an old tradition of children born part-human, part-jaguar.

The fearsome Olmec mask (FIG. 33) is more jaguar than human. The eyes are crossed, the nostrils flared and the mouth squared in a hideous snarl. This mask, hollowed out at the back, was probably worn at some ritual in the cult of the jaguar.

The Olmecs, whose name derives from the word for rubber because they gathered the sticky product of "the weeping trees," are believed to have been the sculptors of the huge stone heads with the thick lips and broad nostrils that were found at La Venta. One weighs 15 tons, others even more. Did the Olmecs who carved heads 8 feet high and 20 feet in circumference, with "crash helmets" for headgear, also make the scary jaguar face masks? And could it

Page 52: COLOR PLATE II   Aztec jadeite seated rabbit, belt decorated with skull and crossbones. Eyes once inlaid. Found at Cempoala, State of Vera Cruz. 1367–1521. 7¼ in. high. Dumbarton Oaks, Washington, D.C., Bliss Collection of Pre-Columbian Art.

have been an Olmec lapidary who carved the head of the woman (FIG. 32) in blue jadeite and endowed her features with all the suffering womankind has known since the race began? This small sculpture, about 2½ inches high, is broken from a figure that might have stood 8 or 9 inches. Superb jadework, yet one doubts that Olmec lapidaries could have torn themselves from their cultural patterns long enough to shape this "Mother of Sorrow." She may have been created at a later time and is Olmec in style only.

"Olmec" inevitably evokes the were-jaguar face. A combination face and tool is the "Kunz adze" (FIG. 34) found in Oaxaca and named for the gemmologist George Frederick Kunz. A votive adze of jadeite (10¹³⁄₁₆ inches long, 6 inches wide and 4⅝ inches thick), it was intended for ceremonial use and not as a working tool. Since it weighs 16 pounds, it could have been employed as a sledge, but such usage would have imperiled the powerful carving. In profile, it shows the typical wedge shape of the adze. Frontally, for more than half its length, it offers a huge, grotesque head, with a puckered mouth and nostrils like blowholes. The short legs are scarcely delineated. Light gray-green with a slight tinge of blue, the jadeite has taken an excellent polish. At the back of the head, a piece of about 2 pounds has been cut away, a mutilation that might have been a ritual "murdering" of the jade when it was placed in a grave. The Kunz adze must have belonged to an important personage or family, for even in raw state a 16-pound block of jade would have cost a great price.

The Olmecs also used jadeite for tooth inlays. However, the examples shown (FIG. 35) are from a set of teeth with green jadeite inlays found in the skull of a Maya priest. A more challenging use for jade is hard to imagine. To shape jadeite for dental fillings, the most exact kind of measurements had to be taken, each cavity had to be drilled precisely, the walls had to be notched and each filling had to be carefully polished or it would never hold. No modern dentist would recommend jade for inlays, for it would wear away the softer natural teeth above or below. However, these inlays were apparently for prestige and decoration only.

Like the Olmec work, Maya jade is to be remembered for its masterpieces. One of the finest is the bluish-green jadeite carved plaque showing a seated Maya dignitary, in audience, or passing judgment on, a lesser figure (FIG. 36). An elaborately embellished bas-relief 5½ inches square, it was probably broken off from a much larger plaque. The larger Maya head—flattened from

FIG. 33   Mask in green jadeite. Hollow back indicates possible use in jaguar cult ceremonies. Olmec, 800–400 B.C. 8¼ × 7⅓ in. Dumbarton Oaks, Washington, D.C., Bliss Collection of Pre-Columbian Art.

FIG. 34   The "Kunz adze." Light greenish-gray jadeite with slight tinge of blue. Said to have
been found in Oaxaca, brought to U.S. about 1890. Olmec, 800–400 B.C. $10\frac{13}{16} \times 6 \times 4\frac{5}{8}$ in.
American Museum of Natural History, New York.

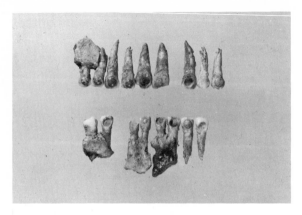

FIG. 35   Maya green jadeite inlays in human teeth. Found in
Guatemala in 1932 (Piedras Negras, Burial No. 5), by University Museum expedition. University Museum, Philadelphia.

babyhood, the hooked nose (perhaps built up with a kind of putty to make it
ceremonially beautiful), the scarified cheeks, with large jade ornaments in the
ear—represents "the true man" of Maya life.

The seated figurine in grayish-green jadeite, 7¼ inches high, of a priest or
god in the round (FIG. 37), clad in a turbanlike headdress with a jewel in its
center, is probably a much earlier Maya work. It sits cross-legged, wears jade
ornaments and has jade disks in the plaited loin belt.

Falling between these two in time is the pale green jadeite pendant (FIG. 38)
with the realistic portrait of a man wearing an elaborate, grotesque headdress
of the Sun God, Kinich Ahau. The eyes of the mask in the headdress are crossed,
in the Maya custom that regarded cross-eyes as beautiful. The face, however,
has a dissipated expression, distaste on its lips, cold disdain in the blank eyes.
Only 3½ inches high, it was found on the breastbones of a skeleton in a tomb
under the West Plaza at Tikal, in 1962, about twelve hundred years after it
left the lapidary's hands.

Since they were all Stone Age people, the Middle Americans' technique
for cutting jade was limited. Sand was the chief abrasive. Possibly, thin slates
wetted and dipped into sand were used to make the initial grooves, although
thin splinters of hardwood might have been just as effective. The first notch
could have been made by stubborn scratching with a sharp-edged obsidian,
and the sawing followed with either slate, or wood, in sand. In some areas,

string-sawing was preferred. A fiber twisted into a string could, when wet with sand, be drawn back and forth like a saw. The worker did not cut all the way through; he turned the piece over and attacked it from the other side too. Midway, a whack with a stick or a stone hammer completed the break.

There were other methods, but all depended on the skill and ingenuity of the individual craftsman. Little drills of bone could make a series of depressions, and the ridges in between would be rubbed down. The Mayas may have used a pump drill. This primitive instrument has a crossbar with a string wound in a direction opposite to that in which the drill will rotate. Depress the

FIG. 36   Bluish-green jadeite plaque: seated Maya dignitary in audience with councillor or captive. Found at Teotihuacán, far from its original home. Probably Late Classic Maya, A.D. 600–900, or earlier. 5½ × 5½ in. The British Museum, London.

crossbar, and by the unwinding of the string, the shaft is forced into a rotary motion. A fine polish could be achieved by rubbing the surface with hematite, which is softer than jadeite, and with a variety of other materials including blocks of wood and hard gourds.

As more and more scientific excavations are made in Middle America, more astonishing jades are uncovered. One day, the jadeite "mines" may be found, but even if great veins should be discovered, their value would be commercial rather than artistic. For no men today can equal the skill of the lapidaries of pre-Columbian times.

Left: FIG. 37 Seated figure in grayish-green jadeite of priest or god. Found at Copan, Honduras. Early Classic Maya, A.D. 300–600. 7 ¼ in. high. The British Museum, London.

Right: FIG. 38 Maya pale green jadeite "portrait" of sun-god Kinich Ahau, carved on pendant. Late Classic Maya, A.D. 600–900. 3 ½ in. high. University Museum, Philadelphia.

CHAPTER IV

Maori

THE MAORIS, A RELATIVELY unsophisticated Polynesian people, were still living in their Neolithic culture when, in the thirteenth or fourteenth century, they left their ancestral homes somewhere in that vast expanse of the South Seas where Tahiti lies. In a fleet of great canoes, they migrated en masse for more than 2,000 miles and settled on the two islands that comprise New Zealand.

We do not know why the Maoris made their exodus, nor why they chose so comparatively cold a site for their new residence. Every element of their earlier adaptation to life in the tropics had to be readapted to make life bearable in the new milieu. They now had to fashion warm garments, build dwellings that could be heated, find food supplies that could be held over through unseasonable times, and construct means of transport that would take them up rivers, upon lakes, into great forests and over towering mountains.

Though primitive by civilized standards, the Maoris were an unusually ingenious people. They were especially gifted in decoration in painting, plaiting, latticework, weaving, tattooing and in carving wood, bone, whale ivory and jade. In every field they had long tradition to guide them—except in the working of jade. The islands from which they had originally come must have lacked an abundant supply of hard stones, at least any as intractable as jade. Now on Mount Cook, which climbs more than 12,000 feet into the New Zealand sky, and elsewhere on the South Island, in the foothills of the adjacent ranges, they discovered the green nephrite, which they named *pounamu*.

Today, scholars believe that jade tools, though rare, could not have been totally unknown in Oceania. Nephrite has been found in New Guinea and in New Caledonia, and jadeite has been located in Celebes. But that does not mean that the Maoris had necessarily encountered the greenstone before, for Oceania is immense. However, once they found jade, they proceeded to employ it for weapons (FIG. 48) and for ornaments. Although they were excel-

FIG. 39   Maori *hei-tiki*, neck pendant in human face. A "male" figure. Green, eyes inlaid with disks of haliotis shell. New Zealand, 18th century or earlier. 3¾ × 2¼ × ¾ in. Buffalo Museum of Science.

lent image-makers in wood, they shaped the nephrite into *hei-tiki* and into minor objects, but never used it for their "god-sticks," and never applied to it those amazingly intricate surface decorations that distinguish most of their artwork—from the prows of their war canoes to the roof beams of their communal houses.

Since the Maoris had no need for a full-scale jade industry, they did not develop one. Weapons for chiefs or headmen required few jade workers, as did the making of those ancestor symbols, the *hei-tiki* neck pendants (FIGS. 39, 40) in which, through successive generations, the *mana*, or prestige, of previous owners accumulated. In the less than five hundred years that the Maoris possessed jade, it nevertheless acquired a special place in their lives. Its sea-green or leaf-green color was appealing; its toughness and hardness made it ideal for war clubs and war picks, and for simple tools like adzes, hoes, chisels and scrapers.

To make a club, or *mere* (FIG. 42), about 10 inches long or more and several inches wide, might occupy a man for three months. Since the Maoris had no metals, they had to cut the pebbles and boulders of nephrite with "saws" of sandstone or thin rock. The artisan, having forced a groove into the *pounamu*, rubbed his saw back and forth in it. He added a little wet quartz sand and repeated the operation again and again. He "sliced" as far as he could and, when he dared, broke pieces off.

The drilling of a hole through which a thong might be pulled took patient labor. The drill, with points of chert or flint, was spun back and forth by rolling between the palms, or perhaps by a simple flywheel attachment. Usually, part of a hole was drilled on one side, the piece turned over and the hole completed by drilling anew on the other side. The shifting drill left countersinkings in the surfaces. The polish was obtained by using more sand, preferably a mixture containing bits of quartz, which is harder than nephrite, and, finally, by

FIG. 40   *Hei-tikis*. Left has toggle and cord, obtained by Capt. James Cook before 1777. Dominion Museum, Wellington. Top and far right, Auckland Institute and Museum. Bottom center, Seattle Art Museum, Eugene Fuller Memorial Collection.

rubbing for hours, sometimes days, with smooth gourds and blocks or leather skins. Fine polishes were effected on ritual or ceremonial weapons and amulets, but most Maori jades, except for the few produced when craftsmanship was at its peak, are not artistic achievements, though some have a rugged charm.

Pounamu was not found everywhere. It was nowhere on the North Island, and only in difficult-to-reach areas on the South Island. One tribe specialized in recovering water-worn nephrite pebbles and boulders from a sea beach and, sometimes, in extracting them from the gravel beds of certain rivers. The finest nephrite was worth the long, difficult journey to Dart Valley near Lake Wakatipu, or to the north Westland district of South Island. Occasionally, there were finds of huge boulders, but these had to be broken down to transportable sizes to be removed and worked. At no time was *pounamu* abundant, and never was good color in ample supply. In recent times, immense pieces of nephrite, the largest estimated at from 2 to 8 tons, have been discovered in the Westland district.

The Maoris appreciated it in any hue and shade, from very light green to very dark green, from the translucent to the opaque. The usual green shade, with small translucent areas, was *kahuraki*; a darker variety was *kawakawa*. The most prized of all, pale green, was *inaka*. Now and then, a yellowish jade was found; more rarely, greens that deepened to bluish tones. Consistency of color and translucence were prized. A small pebble of emerald color, clear as glass, would be valued more than a massive piece of muddy green.

Even among the greenstones, one had to choose carefully. Sometimes *takiwai*, the false nephrite, a variety of serpentine that mineralogists call bowenite, appeared at Anita Bay. It was green enough to catch the eye, soft enough to be cut and shaped by a knife and, at its best, quite attractive. But it was not *pounamu*, the true nephrite jade. The Maoris did not reject the bowenite. They often carved it into fine objects, but they never regarded it as first-class greenstone.

The first amulets were probably made from the smaller pieces of *pounamu* left over from the working of important weapons and tools. A pretty bit of greenstone with unusual color or clarity might be set aside for a chief or a priest, or for some special use. The Maori *hei-tiki*, which is a pendant or amulet in human form, was not intended to express, or copy, ideals of beauty but to indicate the presence of power or personality. The *hei-tiki* (FIG. 40) is like a

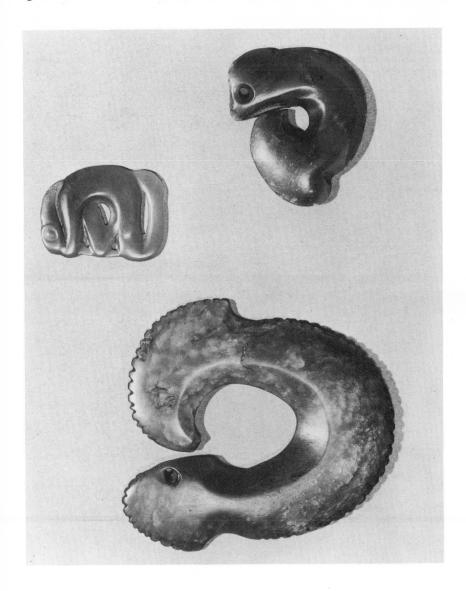

FIG. 41   Maori small green pendants. Two in fishhook form are *hei-matau*; twisted serpent form is *peka-peka*. New Zealand, 18th or 19th century. Museum of Ethnology and Archaeology, Cambridge.

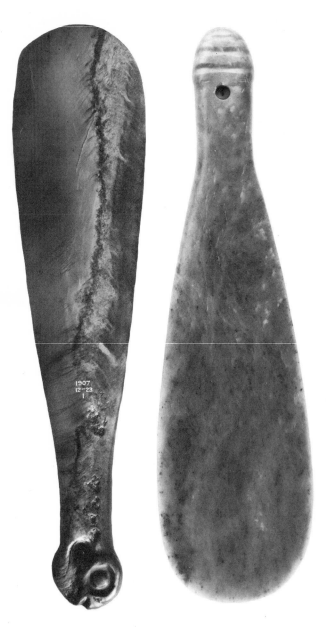

FIG. 42   Maori *mere-pounamu*, short war clubs. New Zealand, 18th century or later. Left, British Museum, London. Right, 16½ × 4½ × ¾ in. Buffalo Museum of Science.

grotesque homunculus, its head twisted to one side, the eyes rimmed red with sealing wax or with inlays of mother-of-pearl. The thighs are spread apart, the knees bent, the soles of the feet touching. Although the *hei-tiki* may be either male or female, scholars are not convinced that it has any fertility significance, or that it is the human embryo in effigy, as has been suggested. Since "tiki" stands for the First Man in Polynesian lore, the little creature may symbolize Man emerging from the primordial dust.

The *mana*, or prestige, of the *hei-tiki*, derives from contact with the important people who owned and wore it. When a person died, it was buried with him. Later, it was withdrawn and worn by son or dear friend, thus serving through another lifetime and gaining *mana* from that contact too, if the new owner was distinguished. The spiritual warmth or presence of those departed, which remained in the *hei-tiki*, made it continuously more valuable as it passed from generation to generation.

The *hei-tiki* is the most important jade object created by the Maoris. Few are more than 7 inches long and few are carved on both sides. Although they all look alike at first glance, close study will reveal differences. Also made of jade were smaller ornaments called *peka-peka* (FIG. 41), some in the shapes of fishes, others like serpents or, at least, spiral-shaped; small amulets in the form of barbs, called *hei-matau*; and random rings and toggles. Since contact with *pounamu* brought benefit to every wearer, one might expect pendants to be made in different forms to please various tastes. However, the range was limited, although any fragment of bright nephrite might be holed, polished a little and worn as a pendant.

As noted before, the Maori talent for intricate ornamentation was never applied to the working of jade. Perhaps the greenstone defeated, or was too unyielding, before Stone Age methods. At the same stage four millennia earlier, the Chinese had developed a jade-cutting industry although they too had lacked metal tools. The Maoris, like the Eskimos and the peoples of the northwest coast of North America, acquired facility in handling jade, but never the skill to embellish it. Unless caches are discovered somewhere in New Zealand, more Maori jades cannot be expected to appear. If any should reach dealers' hands, they will be bought up quickly by museums and collectors. Obviously the supply of *hei-tiki* and other Maori ornaments, amulets, rings and toggles is fast dwindling.

FIG. 43   Eskimo weapons from Alaska. From top: hafted adze, blade of yellow-green jade lashed to caribou-horn handle, Kotzebue Sound. Pale-green knife blade set in horn handle, Cape Nome. 7 ½ × 2 ⅛ in. Skinning and hunting knife blade, translucent gray-green, sharpened along curved edge, Kotzebue Sound. Hunting knife, dull-green blade, 5 ¾ in. long, caribou-horn handle, Bering Coast, Seward Peninsula. Museum of the American Indian, Heye Foundation, New York.

CHAPTER V

Eskimo and Indian

FROM POINT BARROW, well above the Arctic Circle, down to Juan de Fuca Strait north of Puget Sound, from the Mackenzie River basin to the Aleutians, and from the Fraser River and its tributaries to Vancouver Island, the native peoples of Alaska and the northwest coast of North America knew jade from their prehistoric times. However, if their ancestors, when they crossed the Bering Strait from Siberia, had brought an awareness of jade with them, they left their original homes long before jade had become, as with the Chinese, an object of veneration. The Eskimos certainly attached no religious or mythological significance to it. In jade they found a very hard stone that could hold a point or cutting edge much longer than bone or tusk, and they employed it chiefly in tools and weapons.

The Indians of British Columbia may have invented (or retained from some older tradition) a ceremonial, or religious, role for jade. This is suggested by the several unusually large, well-made celts of jade discovered in certain of their burials. Of fine green color, they were in perfect condition, having been finished to some purpose but never put to use. Furthermore, they had been so shaped at both ends that they could not be hafted for either tools or weapons. For what other use could they have been intended except for veneration? *How* they would have been so employed is not clear.

If the Eskimos, or the Tlingit, Haidan, Tsimshian and Kwakiutl Indians, had any esthetic feeling for jade, they showed it only in a sentimental fondness. Jade represented strength and endurance, two attributes those early men required every day in confronting hostile Nature. Jade was shaped into various tools and weapons: knives with fine cutting edges, sharp drill points, sturdy hand hammers, adze blades hafted into caribou rib bones, smooth whetstones, delicate arrow blades, pointed fish barbs, harpoon heads, and war picks. Craftsmanship in jade increased a man's status.

The Eskimos used small sharp pieces to make arming points for their weapons; the others did not. The Eskimos treasured pebbles of good color, especially those with translucent areas, for charms and talismans. The others also appreciated trinkets, but the Eskimos seemed to lavish more affection on their jades and more often used them for personal items.

From jade, the Eskimos fashioned those rare labrets (FIG. 44) that were handed down from generation to generation. The labret was a plug inserted in a hole in the lower lip and worn as a decoration. A tricky object, it consisted, all in one piece, of a lesser button and a larger button, with a slender connecting rod between. The lesser button fit into the opening in the lip and rested securely against the gums; the larger button was to be seen and, presumably, admired. It was easier to carve labrets from ivory, antler or serpentine, but a jade labret was a rare possession.

Neither the Eskimos nor the Indians lacked for the raw materials. The lands that are now Alaska and British Columbia provided ampler supplies of jade than were available at random in Asia. The earliest explorers, beginning with Captain James Cook in 1778, saw greenstone as the cutting element in tools and weapons and recognized it as unusual. Apparently, though, Cook did not realize that this northern greenstone was identical with the *pounamu* he had seen among the Maoris.

When questioned, the Eskimos made no secret of the source of their jade. They said that it came from Jade Mountain. However, explorers were in no haste to journey up the Kobuk River, the 150 miles from Kotzebue Sound,

FIG. 44 Two views of rare jade labret with ornamental groove. Olive-green, fine textured. Found in 1880 in Hotham Inlet, Alaska. Museum of the American Indian, Heye Foundation, New York.

the 40 miles up Shungnak Creek, and then make the hard march to the mountain. But there was no doubt that the mountain existed. In the spring-time, when the snows melted, it lifted its greenish hump more than 1,000 feet against the sky.

In 1885, Lieutenant George M. Stoney of the United States Navy, after several tries, finally reached Jade Mountain. The precise location, 67° 66′ north latitude, 158° 04′ west longitude, is well above the Arctic Circle in the Brooks Range, where the Eskimos had said it was. Since then, dozens of explorers and scientists and countless jade hunters have visited it. Boulders of nephrite in the hundredweight, and up to several tons, have been taken out, broken up and carted away. Only a small percentage of the jade has been of first quality, but enough to make the journey and the hardships worthwhile.

On the other hand, the Indians of the Fraser River basin had no idea of the location of the "mother rock" of their jade. In 1887, George M. Dawson of the Geological Survey of Canada reported quantities of jade on the lower part of the Fraser River, and numerous artifacts of jade in Indian graves. But he found no clue to jade in place. Fifty years later, boulders 10 tons in size were reported. The bedrock source cannot be far away, yet, as of this writing, no one has found it.

The Eskimos seldom made long trips after jade. Decades, perhaps centuries, before their people had gone on such journeys. However, it took weeks by dog-sled and on foot to reach the jade-rich mountain. Perhaps their shamans discouraged them with legends and taboos. Besides, the mountain sent all the jade they could use down into the creekbeds.

There was also a good supply, in middling-size cobbles, on the bars and shallows of the Fraser River. Many crude jade cutting tools (FIG. 43) have been found in the kitchen middens left by the Indians of the Vancouver region. Unlike the Eskimos, who were hunters, these Indians lived by salmon fishing. To work the timbers from which they carved their totem poles, canoes, clubs and masks, they required an abundance of rough tools with sharp cutting edges. For their requirements they needed no refinements, but they encountered the usual difficulties in cutting the greenstone. With a slab of sand schist, they could slice jade by working with a backward-and-forward motion, using fine sand and water for abrasive. With a rotary motion on their sandstone slabs, they could achieve a fair finish and polish. Anyone who is persistent can do it, as Thomas H. Ainsworth, former curator of the Vancouver

City Museum, has so admirably demonstrated for us (FIG. 45).

The Eskimos, who lived in a constant state of warfare with the whale, seal, walrus, polar bear and reindeer, had to approach jade more exactingly. Correctly used, it added power and dimension to Arctic man's small arsenal of implements and pointed weapons. Since his life and his family's food supply might depend on the accuracy of a single throw of a spear or the pitch of a harpoon, he strove to fashion gear that would not fail him. A man's tools and weapons were his most valued possessions. Any dulled or broken jade was carefully cut down to make some smaller object.

Until the Russians, from Siberia, introduced iron tools, the making of a sharp tool or weapon might take weeks. A man bartered such an object only in time of greatest need. Among the Tlingit, a jade adze blade 2 or 3 inches long was worth from one to three slaves. A fine war pick (FIG. 47) became "property" in the best sense, because of its solid merit as a weapon and the pleasure it gave, if only when its owner thought about the many foes it could cut down. An unusual jade article was handed down from chief to chief, or

shared in the family and with one's dearest companions. What could be a better remembrance than a splendid knife or a beautiful harpoon head of jade that once had been carved or used by a deceased friend?

The Eskimos called jade *shungnak* after the creek that flowed from the ribs of Jade Mountain. (Or had the creek been named for *shungnak*, the greenstone?) Among the Salish, jade was *sokala-ist*, which is "green stone," used also to designate green serpentine. The Tlingit called jade *tsu*, simply "green."

The color that appealed most to the Eskimos and the Indians was clear green, the closer to our lettuce-green the more desirable. Even centuries ago, there was probably no lack of "gem-grade" material, that is, fine green and quite translucent. Men had been coming to this area, according to recent researches and carbon-14 dating, as long ago as 8,000 B.C. Onion Portage, near Jade Creek, was a favorite hunting place. While waiting for the herds to come within range, some of the hunters may have walked to Jade Mountain and picked up fine jades.

Twenty-five years ago, a fine high-grade asbestos attracted miners to this

Opposite: FIG. 45   Thomas H. Ainsworth demonstrates how a boulder of jade can be cut by primitive methods. Thomas H. Ainsworth, Vancouver, B.C.

Below: FIG. 46   Eskimo adze and chisel, each set in caribou handle. Lashing of baleen. Found at Kotzebue Sound, Alaska. George Van Hagen, Chicago.

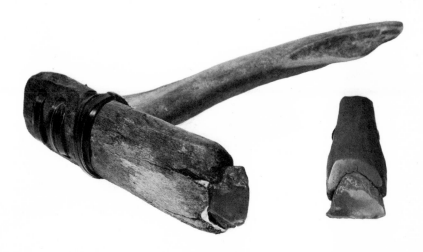

region. Tons of raw jade were taken out incidentally, but much of it was of value only for ordinary carving. If "gem" jades were also found they were put on the market quietly. Over the years, the white men who explored, prospected and settled here probably traded the best jade away from the Eskimos, but these transactions were always private. When a small supply of splendid Alaskan jade did get on the market, some was sent to the Orient, and may have returned to the United States in carved articles as "Chinese" jade.

Today the Eskimos, too, are being "modernized." Men go to Alaska now to drill for oil, but the Jade Mountain area and the Kobuk region continue to attract prospectors. To many it remains one of the most promising sources for jade on the continent, although Wyoming has recently been furnishing the best material, and fine jade can be expected from California. However, Alaska clearly has so much jade that even if only a small percentage proves to be of semiprecious quality, the profits can be considerable. That prospect keeps many jade hunters coming back year after year.

Opposite: FIG. 47 Rare Tlingit war pick,
hafted through end of wooden handle.
Bright green, translucent. Found at Sitka,
Alaska. Blade 16 in. long; handle 23¾ in.
long. United States National Museum,
Washington, D.C.

Above: FIG. 48 Maori "adze of authority."
Long blade tied to handle with carved
human figure, mask carved on pommel below grip. New Zealand, 19th century or
earlier. Dominion Museum, Wellington.

CHAPTER VI

Mughal

TAMERLANE (1336?–1405), WHO IS BURIED under a slab of jade at Samarkand, never achieved his dream of conquering China, but his family, as the Timurids, ruled from the Indus River to the Mediterranean Sea. Accepting Islam, these Mongol peoples also intermarried with the Turks of central Asia. This mixed race of Turko-Mongols we know as the Mughals. Under Babur the Tiger, a descendant of Tamerlane on his father's side and of Genghis Khan on his mother's, the Mughals went south out of Kabul and conquered Hindustan. Mongol—Mogul—Mughal, it is as the latter that their courts are known.

The miniature paintings produced by their artists in illuminating manuscripts became celebrated over the world. The "Mughal" or "Indian" jades, which were created, of course, in lesser number and, naturally, are far costlier, are among the scarcest *objets d'art* known in the West.

Jade must have reached India in earliest times; Turkestan is much closer to northern India than to eastern China. Yet India knew no jade-cutting industry—at least jade does not come into recorded Indian culture—until the Mughals swept down from the northwest and began to devour the native states one by one. By the mid-sixteenth century, when they were in full power, with Akbar as emperor, jade apparently was being carved and appreciated. Not all the Mughal rulers were as magnificently suited to kingship as Akbar, but the Mughal taste for the arts remained even through the reign of the fanatic Aurangzeb and the partition of his empire after he died.

Fortunately, we have jades from the best days, when figures like the builder Shah Jehan raised the gem-studded Peacock Throne, laid out the beautiful Shalimar Gardens at Lahore and constructed the white Taj Mahal at Agra as a mausoleum for Queen Mumtaz. It was for Shah Jehan that the nephrite cup with ibex-head handle was made (FIG. 49). We even know when, for an

---

FIG. 49   Mughal wine cup in form of gourd with ibex head. Translucent white. Probably carved in India. Dated for our year 1657. 2½ × 7½ in. Victoria and Albert Museum, London.

inscription engraved in a small cartouche on the cup gives the Shah's titles and a Muslim date that corresponds to our year 1657.

The cup, 7½ inches wide by 2½ inches high, is carved of the finest white nephrite in the shape of half a gourd, with four lobes gracefully narrowing toward the neck, where the head of the ibex forms, with spiraled, curved horns, little beard and slightly parted jaws. The gourd rests on an up-ended lotus blossom that can be seen only when the cup is turned over. Six lotus petals, curved and open, make a footing for the piece, while, from beneath, acanthus leaves arrow out and cover the underparts of the lobes. The lapidary hollowed out the vessel and abraded the nephrite to transparent thinness.

It was regarded as a masterpiece in its own time, or it would not have been graced with Shah Jehan's name and titles. Other jades, a jug and several coupes, or drinking vessels, also carry Jehan's inscriptions. All are elegantly hollowed to shell-thin transparency and polished to rare smoothness. Nothing like them—certainly nothing like the cup with ibex-head handle—ever issued from China. In fact, no jades from China ever surpassed the Mughal pieces in sophistication of design and execution. Yet the tradition is that the first jade craftsmen in India were imported from China. If that is true, then the immigrant carvers trained groups of native lapidaries.

There was, however, more than a difference in sophistication between the Chinese and the Indian carvings. To the Chinese, the jade itself had been of first importance. Its substance was all; therein lay its virtue. And substance included color, imperfections, opaqueness or translucence, and the form into which it was wooed. Add the subtle bond between venerated object and venerating person—and only then can the relationship of the Chinese lapidary to jade be fully understood.

To the Mughal, or Indian, connoisseur, jade at its finest was precious indeed, but it was one more precious stone in a land overflowing with precious stones. All mystic feeling for jade was absent. Gems had never attracted the Chinese fancy and ornate jewelry was little appreciated until the late Ming dynasty. However, the Mughals and, of course, the native Indian patrons, who were accustomed to lavish decor, expected to see gems everywhere. Why not, also, on the soft, limpid tints of nephrite, which, white or green, offered such a splendid background for precious stones? The new jade-cutting industry produced great numbers of simple jades, but the Delhi school developed a style of gem-encrusting on jade that became a distinctive Hindu specialty.

Above: FIG. 50 Mughal dagger handle in shape of horse's head. Blue-gray, inlaid with gold traceries; rubies, or red stones, for the eyes and in the rosettes. India, 18th century. 5 in. high. Victoria and Albert Museum, London.

FIG. 51 Mughal mirror-back with pierced crown and cut-out design of flowers. The front (not shown) is set with 82 small cabochon rubies, each in a gold bezel. White, with faint yellowish tinge. India, 17th century. 6⅜ × 4 in. Seattle Art Museum, Eugene Fuller Memorial Collection.

Rubies, sapphires, emeralds, garnets, tourmalines, pearls, turquoises and even diamonds, each set in a little cloison, or cell, of gold or silver, were used to invest the jades with new charm.

The stones, rising scarcely a millimeter above the surface, had to be cemented in firmly, so narrow grooves and channels were incised to accommodate them. Thus, the new jades required firm walls to hold the gold and silver traceries, the gemstones, and the cloisonné enamels that were occasionally employed. This necessity signaled the end of the eggshell-thin jades. All jeweled jades are half again as thick as the translucent cups and jugs that bear Shah Jehan's name.

Undeniably, the new Mughal pieces represented a technical advance over the Chinese jades. The Hindu lapidaries had surpassed their Chinese teachers and the tactile quality they brought to the surfaces of their jades was never excelled. Obviously, only a limited number of patrons could afford the jeweled jades, but only a limited number of craftsmen had the fine skill needed to create them—and these masters seldom worked alone. A designer, a carver and a jewelsmith usually worked together, although a jewelsmith might also design his own pieces. Each team probably employed apprentices for the minor chores. The finished products were, strictly speaking, *jewels* rather than jades.

Once the jewelsmiths learned to subdue jade they gave their ingenuity full play. They mitered panels and fitted them together so cleverly for jewel boxes, brush boxes and presentation boxes that the eye could not detect the places of joining. They hollowed out teapots (FIG. 52) as easily as small medicine vials and furnished close-fitting covers. They pierced jade at fifty points, as in the mirror-back (FIG. 51), drilled, cut under and came up again, and executed designs that interlaced palmettes, lotuses and grapevines. They made plates like open chrysanthemums, with a hundred slender petals lapping and overlapping, each alive with its own rhythm. Rosettes, ferns, stars, buds, leaves, all appeared and reappeared in formal arrangements, or in cunningly asymmetrical ones, yet never became tiresome. To such masterful skill with jade, add the harmonies derived from the rich reds, soft greens and slender golds of the gemstones and the precious metals.

The popular sword or dagger hilts (FIG. 50), shaped to fit the hand, were wound with ribands of enamels and studded with gems. Little jade wine cups bore miniature portraits of the Mughal emperors, with Cufic inscriptions entwined in arabesques from which rubies and emeralds depended like tiny grapes. White jade snuff bottles were made to shimmer in a gossamer of rose-diamonds and sapphires, with, as a final touch, a cabochon ruby atop the stopper. Necklaces of jade beads were embellished with white nephrite pendants suspended from braided gold cords, each pendant adorned with gold and pearls, turquoises and rubies.

With the arrogance of the supremely accomplished, the lapidaries seemed to plead for more difficult assignments. To protect a Koran or an album of miniatures, they produced book covers of jade, carving sage-green nephrite panels with openwork designs (vines, diapers and arabesques), then bordering each panel with a white jade frame, which in turn was enclosed in a sage-green rim. The spine might be graced with a chain of five medallions, while gold-pinned hinges held the front and back covers.

Certain of the Mughal masterpieces reached Peking. The imperial work-shops, which had once absorbed all the fine jade mined in Turkestan, or fished

FIG. 52   Mughal teapot with inlays of jewels and red enamel celled in gold. Dark green. India, 17th century. 4¼ in. high. Victoria and Albert Museum, London.

from its rivers, had been aware that high-quality nephrite was being diverted to India. The Chinese craftsmen themselves had not totally rejected the idea of pure decoration. As early as the Chou and Han dynasties they had inlaid bronze buckles, girdle hooks, dagger hilts and even large vases with gold and silver ornaments, and with malachite and turquoise. Jade, glass and crystal had sometimes been used to embellish gilt bronze furnishings and appliqués. However, precious stones were hardly ever employed. In the Ming era, the vogue for artistic confections in jewelry had spread, but the Chinese pieces, elaborately designed, were nonetheless ethereal in feeling and seldom barbarously rich.

The imperial craftsmen received the Indian productions with curiosity and good humor rather than envy. They tried their hands at the Mughal style, but with reservations. They were not moved to repeat the intricate inlays, but perhaps were inspired by them to create elaborate jade trees, with leaves and petals of jade combined with coral, agate and carnelian, which they "planted" in cloisonné enamel pots. They refrained from fixing gemstones everywhere.

Responding, however, to the foreign interest in the new jades, a separate branch of the imperial workshops deliberately set out to imitate them. Cut in the "Indian school," these jades are admirable facsimiles, some so emphatically Mughal in feeling that only the imperial mark—many bear the cachet of Ch'ien-lung—reveals that Chinese hands created them. Chinese or Indian, "Mughal" jades today command the highest prices and are quite beyond the reach of most collectors.

FIG. 53   Long-handled Mughal spoon with gold and gilt bronze inlays. Skim-milk white with gray-green tinge. India, 17th century. 10¼ in. long. Seattle Art Museum, Gift of Mr. and Mrs. James D. Burns.

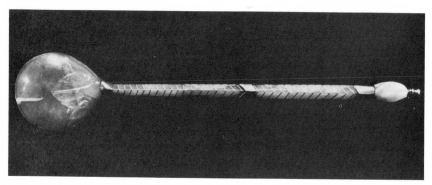

CHAPTER VII

Advice to the Collector

1. *See all the jade you can.* The nearest science or natural history museums offer mineralogy exhibits that display nephrite and jadeite. Observe the "raw" minerals and note the differences between them. If you prefer finished work, visit art museums to see the carved jades. Enjoy the colors.

2. Note the difference between the old Chinese carvings and the modern work. The latter, though they may be technically superb, lack the spirit of the earlier craftsmanship. Observe how the "archaic" jades, though many have lost their original colors, have retained their noble styling.

3. Observe the crude Eskimo and Northwest Coast jades. These tools and weapons of nephrite lack sophistication, yet they possess the strength of objects that have been well-used.

4. See Maori jades. These, too, are of nephrite. Though *hei-tikis* may repel, they were greatly revered. Since the Maori pieces may be the scarcest, no serious collector should forego an opportunity to acquire Maori jade.

5. The jadeites of the Aztecs and the Mayas often have extraordinary appeal and have a unique vitality. The jadeite masks and figures are far rarer than the Chinese nephrites. They seem more "Western," as if the men who carved them saw the world as we do.

6. Modern jades, especially those now carved from American finds by hobbyists, or by professional lapidaries, can be very attractive. Figures and animals are still produced in the Fabergé tradition, but not often are they as delightfully carved as they were in the days of Carl Peter Fabergé.

7. There are many imitations of jade. So be careful if the piece is costly, and even if it is not. Note also that much dyed jade is on the market today. Therefore for the average collector, the rule had better be: *Caveat emptor!*

Repeat: See all the jade you can. You should have some jade of your own, to hold, to fondle, to study closely. One day you may own beautiful and rare jades. Since jade is the study and the pleasure of a lifetime, why not begin now?

SELECTED BIBLIOGRAPHY

BARROW, T. *The Decorative Arts of the New Zealand Maori*. Wellington, New Zealand: A. N. & A. W. Reed, 1964.

DIGBY, ADRIAN. *Maya Jades*. London: The British Museum, 1964.

EMMONS, GEORGE T. *Jade in British Columbia and Alaska, and Its Use by the Natives*. Monograph No. 35 in the Indian Notes and Monograph Series. New York: Museum of the American Indian, Heye Foundation, 1923.

FOSHAG, WILLIAM F. *Mineralogical Studies on Guatemalan Jade*. Publication 4307. Washington, D.C.: Smithsonian Institution, 1957.

HANSFORD, S. HOWARD. *Chinese Jade Carving*. London: Lund Humphries & Co., 1950.

KRAFT, JAMES LEWIS. *Adventure in Jade*. New York: Henry Holt, 1947.

LAUFER, BERTHOLD. *Jade: A Study in Chinese Archaeology and Religion*. Publication 154, Anthropological Series, Vol. X. Chicago: Field Muusem of Natural History, 1912.

LOTHROP, S.K. "Jade and String Sawing in Northeastern Costa Rica." In *American Antiquity*, Vol. 21, No. 1, July 1955, pp. 43–51.

NOTT, STANLEY CHARLES. *Chinese Jade Throughout the Ages: A Review of Its Characteristics, Decoration, Folklore and Symbolism*. London: B. T. Batsford, 1936.

RUFF, ELSIE. *Jade of the Maori*. London: Gemmological Association of Great Britain, 1950.

SAVAGE, GEORGE. *Chinese Jade: A Concise Introduction*. New York: October House, 1965.

WHITLOCK, H. P. and EHRMANN, M. L. *The Story of Jade*. New York: Sheridan House, 1949.

FIG. 54   Chinese mask of human face, perhaps an amulet. Creamy nephrite, some corrosion. Shang. 1 ¾ × 1 ⁵⁄₁₆ × ⁹⁄₁₆ in. Nelson Gallery—Atkins Museum, Kansas City.